Teaching American History:

AN INQUIRY APPROACH

AVRAM BARLOWE

ANN COOK: SERIES EDITOR

TEACHERS COLLEGE PRESS

COMMUNITY STUDIES, INC Ⓢ

Grateful acknowledgement to the Bill and Melinda Gates Foundation and Community Studies, Inc. for support provided

Distributed by Teachers College Press, 1234 Amsterdam Avenue, New York, NY 10027

ISBN 0-8077-4560-X

Manufactured in the United States of America

11 10 09 08 07 06 05 04   8 7 6 5 4 3 2 1

CONTENTS

Introduction

Not long ago, I began a high school course I was teaching in the history of the Civil Rights Movement by asking students to fill in a timeline of important twentieth century events. I did this partly to draw their attention to a larger context for the period we would be studying as well as to determine what understanding they had of historical context. I supplied them with a list of fifteen major developments ranging from World War I to the election of George W. Bush and instructed them to write in these items along with appropriate dates on the timeline.

A majority of students in my school are transfers from other institutions. This particular class of twenty-five students was a mix of sophomores, juniors, and seniors. Nearly every one of them had taken American history courses covering the twentieth century at either or both the junior high and high school level. Very few, however, could place more than three or four of the events in their proper places and most had no overall sense of the events' chronology. Especially telling was the fact that while almost none could properly place Pearl Harbor in the overall chronology, most were able to identify December 7th as the date when the Japanese military had attacked Pearl Harbor. But the year eluded them. Guesses ranged from as close as the 1940s to as far away as 1917. When informed that the correct answer was 1941, many responded that the bombing of Hiroshima must have occurred in the following year, bringing an end to the war.

Apparently, sound bites such as December 7th had registered in their consciousness far more strongly than had the meaning or historical context, yet another indication of American history teaching's failure to develop students' broader historical awareness.

This was not unusual. Americans' understanding of both our nation's history and our country's relationship to the world at large has become a major public concern. The charge that our students know too little about their past has assumed a prominent place on the long list of criticisms routinely directed at the state of American education.

The enduring problem of historical ignorance raises serious questions about why such an unsuccessful approach to teaching has persisted. If we are truly interested in developing educated citizens who can use historical knowledge to function more effectively in the current world and to participate in the democratic process, perhaps we need an approach that puts the emphasis on argument rather than information—a process that could involve students in historical inquiry and debate while simultaneously refining the skills they need to do this at increasingly sophisticated levels.

James Loewen describes the broad outlines of such an approach in the national bestseller *Lies My Teacher Told Me*. In contrast to summary survey courses, he argues that teachers must focus on fewer topics that are examined more thoroughly, and he emphasizes that the investigation of the selected topics must focus on historical controversy in a manner that encourages students to disagree as long as they can "back up their disagreement with serious historical work: argumentation based on evidence." He calls for more independent student research from a variety of sources, including libraries, journals, books, and people in the community who are connected to historical events. Finally, Loewen urges teachers and students to interrogate all sources, posing a set of questions designed to help students assess their validity, integrity, and point of view.

Because Loewen's guidelines assume depth, controversy, and student input in the shaping of the curriculum, they cannot be translated into a blueprint that details every activity, assignment, and question and assume interested teachers will copy them. On the contrary, the guidelines require a pedagogical framework best provided by an inquiry approach to teaching and learning. Thus, an understanding of the inquiry teaching method must precede any description of an alternative American history curriculum.

The inquiry method, which is the foundation of my own work, views student interest, understanding, experience and viewpoint as crucial to the assimilation of academic content. It assumes that students' accumulation of information is relatively useless unless students can articulate and reflect on that information from their own point of view. In an inquiry setting students must define and understand the material being examined and be allowed to evaluate and interpret it on their own terms and on the basis of their own experience.

AVRAM BARLOWE

1   The Inquiry Approach

Inquiry prizes the individual student's process and experience, not for inherent truth or clarity, but because process and experience together represent the student's way of thinking. Inquiry contends that the learner cannot transcend the limitations of his thinking by replacing his thought process with someone else's. Inquiry teaching insists that development occurs best when an original thought system is expanded—that meaningful learning happens when students begin with their own perspectives and then refine or modify them through discussion with others. If a student's search for meaning is regarded by a teacher as "wrong," the learning process is undermined.

In contrast to textbook-driven teaching, inquiry teachers strive to create an environment in which students learn in a context they help to create. Instead of scripting predetermined questions and answers in the manner of traditional lesson plans, inquiry teachers encourage students to explain things as they see them and then to support and expand those explanations using evidence. Inquiry teachers guide students through a personal and collective process of trial and error enriched by techniques designed to confront and enlarge their thinking. Within the confines of a given theme or subject, inquiry teachers present or ask students to locate relevant information. They then initiate activities designed to develop strategies and skills for comprehending and analyzing the information so that students can think, say, and write something that synthesizes their individual perspective with a general knowledge of the material.

If the topic, for example, is the role played by George Washington in the American Revolution, the student will not be asked merely to describe his work as commander of the Continental Army, his relationship to the Continental Congress, or his assumption of the Presidency after the war. Instead, students in an inquiry class will be asked to marshal and present such information as it relates to their assessment of Washington's role. The relevant historical details will of course be a vital part of what is said and written, insofar as those details serve as evidence to support or clarify the students' views about Washington's impact.

The writing, reading, and thinking skills in inquiry classroom activities support the growth of this synthesis of evidence and personal knowledge. Students are encouraged to articulate their reactions and interpretations of the material being examined in their classes. Through discussion, debate, interviews with guests, written exchanges, and critiques of each other's work, they are pressed to expand these interpretations, to go beyond comfortable generalizations and to substantiate their ideas with ever expanding evidence. Together with their classmates, students create and recreate criteria by which they evaluate the often-conflicting perspectives brought to the classroom by different students.

TEACHER'S ROLE

The teacher guides this work. While certainly aware of and prepared for the terrain she wants to cover and issues she hopes will arise, she must also guard against asking questions that lead students to a particular conclusion or point of view. Rather, questions must be designed to evoke discussion and exchange. Once that occurs, the teacher's job is to maintain a central focus, scaffold and represent ideas and disagreements, clarify ambiguities, permit appropriate digressions, incorporate new questions, insist on support for arguments, and introduce relevant questions and evidence if and when that is appropriate. This requires teachers to listen carefully to what students are saying and to organize discussion and student work in a coherent but somewhat improvised manner. Over time, teachers develop these skills and accumulate the wide range of resources needed to conduct inquiry classes.

In the interest of promoting an inquiry environment, an American history curriculum focuses its courses on an in-depth examination of a few central topics. Rather than race through three or four hundred years of our nation's past in a superficial manner, an entire four- or five-month term is devoted to one, two or three of the following topics: European exploration and colonization, the American Revolution, the U.S. Constitution, slavery in the United States, the Civil War, Reconstruction, westward expansion, U.S.-Latin American relations at the turn of the 20th Century, World War I, migration and immigration, the Great Depression, World War II, the Cold War, Vietnam, and the Civil Rights Movement.

To some extent, such in-depth teaching means losing a certain degree of perspective. The student who chooses, for example, in two different semesters to study the American Revolution and the Vietnam War may lack a specific understanding of how U.S. intervention in Cuba in 1898 anticipated America's involvement in Southeast Asia years later. What is gained, however, is an approach to historical issues. Having considered some thorny historical questions in detail, having weighed conflicting interpretations on the basis of evidence, having reacted to arguments about war and revolution through the prism of his own experience, this student is more likely to develop or incorporate that way of thinking and knowledge than the student in the survey course who has a shallow grasp of all three events, provided he can even remember them. (Certainly, if the New York State High School Regents Exam is a valid guide, there is no indication that students exposed to a traditional curriculum are expected to make connections at the level indicated here.)

A brief survey of a semester-long American history course that I've taught should illustrate this claim. In addition to presenting teacher-generated materials, it will also highlight the role played by students in shaping the curricular focus of an inquiry course since questions, resources, and activities may vary each time it is taught.

Introducing the American Revolution

In most high school classrooms the American Revolution is presented as a glorious, hallowed but rather predictable affair in which a wise and benevolent group of Founding Fathers leads a united colonial people in a struggle against royal tyranny, thereby creating a new, democratic form of government. This scenario is reinforced by the images of the Revolution (e.g., Washington crossing the Delaware, men in wigs and stockings signing the Declaration of Independence, Paul Revere on horseback) that dominate the textbooks and remain in students' consciousness long after memories of dates and places have faded. While not without truth, such a scenario disregards a fight for independence that was a complex drama of conflicting interests that persist in America today. It thus denies students an opportunity to reflect on dynamic issues and tensions that are a recognizable part of their lives and to view the Revolution as a vibrant legacy. The result is that students tend to see it as a bland event far removed from their experience.

This alienation, however, can be a very useful starting point from which a historical investigation can proceed. For even within the confines of received wisdom there are variations and different degrees of understanding that can serve as a vehicle for further inquiry. Thus, the first order of business in an inquiry course on the American Revolution is to place student opinions at the center of discussion by asking the kids to tell each other what, if anything, they already know about this event and to identify the questions that their mistakes and disagreements inevitably generate.

I begin this by asking students to write for five or ten minutes in response to the following questions:

> What was the American Revolution?
> Why did it happen?
> Who supported it? Who opposed it?

As I distribute the worksheet containing these questions I explain to students that it is not a quiz, but rather an activity designed to raise questions about the Revolution by sharing and discussing what we already know. This means that their answers will not be marked right or wrong and that whatever information they reveal in writing will not be identified as theirs unless they choose to do so. I collect their responses and read them aloud, usually four or five at a time, asking students to comment on each other's answers and explain why they agree or disagree with them. I also encourage them to raise questions about the Revolution that occur to them during these exchanges. An extended or especially lively disagreement will be summarized in the form of a question so that by the end of the discussion the class has accumulated a list of questions for further exploration. A recent list included the following:

> Was England oppressing all of the colonists?
> Did colonists who didn't pay taxes care about the fight with England?
> What kind of freedom were the colonies fighting for?
> Was slavery an issue in the revolution?

These questions vary each time the class is taught, depending upon the dimensions of the discussion. There is, however, always the expectation that we will return repeatedly to these questions during the course of the semester as our deeper exploration unfolds. Occasionally I type up the written responses for students to read and discuss in a following class. I reproduce this work in order to present their ideas as text. This begins the process of demystifying the written word and helps students focus more closely.

These written responses to questions about the Revolution are either followed or preceded by a "pre-test" that asks students to identify major names and events associated with the Revolution. In this exercise students grade their own exams, share answers in small groups, and save or dispose of them as they see fit. The main purpose of this pre-test is to determine what they already know as a class and to establish a yardstick against which they can measure their knowledge at the end of the term.

Another issue that I like to have students examine early in the course (and periodically return to over the course of the semester) is the definition of the word "revolution." I provide them with an assignment that presents brief descriptions of important historical changes in world history (e.g., the Civil War, the Nat Turner rebellion, the end of communist rule in East Germany, the New Deal, the "sexual revolution" of the 1960s, the French Revolution) and ask them whether or not each selection describes a revolution and why. In the discussion that follows students argue about their answers and often offer conflicting definitions of revolution.

3 The Declaration of Independence

Following the opening activities, the focus usually turns to a primary source—the Declaration of Independence—to answer questions about the nature and causes of the American Revolution. Each student is given a copy of the document, an extensive glossary to help him or her negotiate its rather difficult vocabulary, and a homework assignment that asks students to rewrite the first two paragraphs of the Declaration in their own words. They are asked as well to explain what those paragraphs tell them about why the American Revolution happened, who supported and opposed it, and they are asked to identify important ideas they agree or disagree with.

In class, students are divided into groups of two or three and asked to compare their translations, perhaps construct a group one, and take note of any significant disagreements they had about its meaning. A full group discussion of the answers then follows, focusing on those parts of the Declaration that provide answers to our earlier questions and raise new questions such as:

- What did the authors mean when they said "all men are created equal"?
- Does the decision to overthrow a government rest mostly on how much suffering people can take?
- Who wrote and signed this document and did they speak for everyone involved in the Revolution?

- How many Americans actually read the Declaration of Independence or heard it read?

It is possible at this point to move on to an examination of the grievances that follow the Declaration's opening paragraphs. I sometimes ask students to indicate which group or groups of Americans they think each grievance speaks for and, using the grievances as evidence, to describe three reasons that the Revolution happened. We might also explore how well the Declaration answers some of the questions students have generated. However, such an exercise involves using fairly difficult and somewhat obscure texts to ascertain much of the Revolution's action and development. Therefore, I usually prefer to wait until students have greater familiarity with important background information.

SECONDARY SOURCES

Having digested some of the Declaration in its original form, it is important for students to begin viewing the document in a broader context. This work requires students to absorb and evaluate what contrasting secondary sources have to say about the document. The examination of primary and secondary sources brings a dimension to student understanding that is lacking in the standard textbook approach to teaching and it is a pattern used throughout inquiry-based courses.

Though not used in a traditional fashion, textbooks can be a valuable tool. Over the years I have collected a wide variety of textbook descriptions of the Declaration. As one might expect, analyses of the Declaration appearing forty years ago differ considerably from those that are more current. Typically, I assemble three or four sources, making sure to include both more and less demanding selections. I ask students to read them, highlight important information discussed in each selection, write about how the sources differ on key issues and which source they feel is the most accurate and why. They must also note any answers the sources provided to the ongoing question of why the Revolution occurred.

This assignment prepares students to consider conflicting positions in a discussion of the Declaration and the Revolution and to use evidence to support their points of view. Depending upon the students' responses to the readings, the discussion may focus on the power of the Declaration's ideas, the meaning of equality to the men who signed it, the role it played in mobilizing colonial society, the impact it had on the broader populace, or the specific grievances that impelled it. Whatever the particular issue, I encourage students to address it from their own, often differing perspectives and to use available evidence to support their views and raise additional, relevant questions.

The Missing Slavery Clause

READING, DISCUSSION, WRITING

If the equality issue and its slavery subtext are particularly compelling, I often introduce a follow-up assignment on the Declaration's deleted or modified slavery clause. Frequently ignored by most traditional texts, this clause was originally one of the Declaration's many grievances against the English King. It holds the King responsible for the introduction of the colonial slave trade, which it condemns for its horrifying impact on the colonies' African population. The assignment asks students to read the clause and, with the aid of a glossary, to rewrite it in their own words. It also requires them to read two or three short accounts of the clause's inclusion and deletion, to use evidence gleaned from their explanation of its deletion, and to reflect on whether the Continental Congress made the right decision in deleting it. In the class that follows this assignment, students, in either small groups or in the class as a whole, compare their "translations." Frequently, they will spend considerable time arguing over the passage's literal meaning and Jefferson's and the other signers' definition of "equality" and their attitudes towards African Americans. Students then evaluate the different interpretations of the political struggle surrounding the clause and debate the decision to delete it. They inevitably raise questions about the meaning of freedom in this Revolution that are, in my view, essential to an understanding of it.

Students frequently show an intense interest in this issue, and I am then faced with a decision about whether to pursue it more deeply or to move on to a direct investigation of the origins and evolution of the Revolution. My decision is based on an assessment of how much prerequisite information about the Revolution and how much additional academic support students need to engage materials connected with this issue. For example, will students be able to evaluate the evidence supporting Gary Nash's claim that South Carolina and Georgia could not have afforded to bolt from the United States over the slavery issue? My decision must also hinge on a judgment of how much total ground must be covered for students to gain a reasonable, overall understanding of the Revolution and how much broader information can be absorbed through an investigation of a narrower issue. How worthwhile is it, for example, to jump into the Dunmore Proclamation (an offer of freedom made to slaves willing to enlist in the British Army prior to the Declaration) or Washington's evolving attitude toward African-American participation in the Continental Army? Both topics offer an opportunity to broaden students' understanding of the context in which the Declaration addressed equality and slavery and to explore the interests that varying social groups had in the revolutionary process. On the other hand, there are limits to examining them without an awareness of important events that preceded them. In an inquiry framework, digression and deeper exploration help give students ownership of the learning process, but the teacher's role is to weigh this input alongside other academic needs and concerns.

An examination of the Declaration can also involve a look at the Declaration's influence on other historical American documents and events. The class can compare the Declaration with the Seneca Falls Sentiments and many other protest documents that have used it as a model. It can respond to Frederick Douglass's analysis of July 4th and its meaning to the slave. It can assess the merits of John Lewis's March on Washington contention that the Civil Rights Movement reflects the Declaration's spirit.

Activities

Before proceeding to an examination of the social and political events that led to the Declaration, I usually involve students in a map exercise designed to familiarize them with the Revolution's geographical and geopolitical dimensions. Rather than present them with information to be memorized, I provide students with a map of North America circa 1763 that includes the thirteen colonies' geographic borders but does not identify any of them by name. I ask each student to fill in the blank spaces with the name of each colony and then to produce a second map of this kind with other students in small groups. When these tasks are completed, I give each group a "correct" copy of the map and have the groups grade the maps they have produced. I then open up a discussion based upon the additional questions that are invariably raised (e.g., Why weren't Florida and Maine original British colonies? Why did France control the land west of the Mississippi? Which colonies had slavery? Why do some Canadians speak French if England controlled Canada at this point?) I usually answer these questions directly, but sometimes, if the exchanges surrounding a question are particularly compelling, I help the students research that question. The entire map-making process allows students to add what they already know to the class's information base, to share any embarrassments they might have about things they don't know, and to work together to advance their collective wisdom.

Traditionally, students are introduced to events such as the Stamp Act or the Boston Massacre through the reading of a textbook chapter that links descriptions of these events to the larger "story" of the Revolution. They then typically analyze these events by answering questions at the chapter's end and responding to classroom materials and activities that advance teacher-driven interpretations. This process usually results in their acceptance of a conventional historical narrative that emphasizes national political unity, a homogenized American identity, and the leadership of colonial elites. Even when that is not the case, even when a more critical or skeptical view is presented, it is usually not done in an open-ended manner that invites student input. In contrast, my American History course is designed to expose students to a variety of narratives and to encourage them to create their own.

Before exposing students to any particular narrative or engaging them in an in-depth examination of the events that led to revolutionary war, I prefer first to familiarize them with the broad outline of these events and allow them to construct their own, rough sense of their relation. They do this through an inquiry technique known as a "sort." Students are given a chronology comprising brief descriptions of specific developments in England and the Americas in the period leading up the signing of the Declaration. They are asked to "sort out" what *they think* are the five events or developments that most contributed to the eventual Declaration of Independence, to explain in writing why *they think* each of their chosen events was important, and to write down any questions they now have about these events or the Revolution in general. They may also be asked to explain what, if anything, their chronology choices tell them about why the Revolution occurred, who supported and who opposed it. This work can be done individually at home or in the classroom.

Upon completion of the assignment students are placed in small groups in which they examine each other's choices and come up with a group-derived choice of the three events which most contributed to American independence. They are asked as well to write up a brief explanation of why they made these choices. The small group process allows students to discuss, defend, and reflect on their choices in a more direct and personal setting. Group choices and an abbreviated version of their explanations are rewritten on the classroom blackboard. The groups then present their choices and respond to questions, comments and disagreements from other students. This full group discussion also addresses ongoing questions about the Revolution's character and causes. There are invariably differences between students who stress oppressive English legislation and those who stress colonial resistance, between those who emphasize violent conflicts and those who cite the power of ideas, and between those who point to economic contradictions and those impressed by political ones.

The exchanges surrounding the group choices highlight issues and events that the class wants to investigate more closely and generate a host of new inquiry tasks and questions. The teacher's job at this point is to make her own hard choices about the options within this framework and the depths to which they will be pursued. It is important, for example, to focus on events that spark lively debate or generate wide interest, but it important as well to ensure that the events and questions selected capture what the teacher thinks is essential. In this sense, the teacher's narrative of the Revolution, while not imposed, is not irrelevant.

6   The Mother Country

Whatever the focus of student interest in a given term, I like first to equip them with a basic understanding of the colonies' relationship to the British mother country. I tend to introduce this with the Navigation Acts, which shed considerable light on colonial economics. These laws, easily read in their original language, are fairly straightforward descriptions of what the colonies can and cannot produce and under what conditions they may buy and sell in the open market. Students can read them individually, collectively, or in small groups and debate what these regulations tell them about the colonial relationship and who benefited from it. This process, which allows them to interpret the varying dimensions of British control, provides them with a much more accessible and fluid comprehension of colonial economics than a textbook summary might.

It is also important for students to grasp the nature of the colonies' political relationship with England, which was far more complex than mere obedience to a king. British rule in North America involved an elaborate mixture of formal democracy, popular autonomy, and imperial dictate that is often ignored or inadequately explained in conventional texts. I prefer to convey this information to students in a manner that clearly identifies the various decision-makers and their connection, but allows them to expand their own definitions of the colonial relationship and to revisit the matter of why the Revolution occurred and who supported and opposed it. I provide them with charts I have devised that diagram the state's legislative and executive processes in both England and the colonies.

The charts include information on the different branches of government and the requirements for holding office and voting. They are given to students within the context of a brief lecture that explains how political decisions were made and who made them. Students are encouraged to raise and debate questions during the course of the lecture.

My primary interest here is to provide them with background they will need to assess the political struggles that culminated in a revolutionary break. However, I also want them to reflect on the colonies' social composition and the development and meaning of democracy in America. Their responses to the charts generally enable students to do that. In general, they react strongly, but not uniformly, to the fact that property requirements placed limits on the kind of people who could participate in formal government. (Discussion of this issue sometimes leads to research focused on economic divisions in colonial society and the average yearly incomes of various economic groups.) At the same time, they develop an appreciation of the situation that faced property holding voters and officials in their conflict with the Parliament and the King.

I sometimes find it useful at this point to have students compare the situation of England's thirteen North American colonies in the 18th Century with the situation of Puerto Rico today. Students peruse another chart that contrasts the political and economic rights of colonial Americans in relation to England with those of Puerto Rico's current residents in relation to the continental United States. They then discuss the ways in which they think the relationships are similar and different and whether or not one set is preferable to the other. My purpose here is not to publicize Puerto Rican grievances or to promote Puerto Rican independence, but rather to strengthen students' grasp of colonialism by having them compare the past to the present.

7   The People

The place of the disenfranchised colonial masses in the revolutionary struggle is rarely explored or appreciated at the high school level. Most textbooks present these people as vaguely democratic appendages of dynamic political leaders such as Sam Adams, Paul Revere, and Patrick Henry. (Even the treatment of newly discovered "heroes" such as Crispus Attucks reflects this approach.) However, recent historical scholarship reveals that crowds of ordinary people—what John Adams labeled "the motley crew"—played an active and purposeful role in colonial society and politics before and throughout the period of revolutionary struggle. The struggles surrounding the Stamp Act, which invariably find a place on students' most important lists, offer a perfect opportunity for students to begin an exploration of this phenomenon.

PRIMARY SOURCES
THE STAMP ACT

This unit begins with an examination of the Stamp Act itself. The statute's essential features are included in an excerpt that is twenty-five lines long and the addition of an eight-word glossary makes it relatively easy to read. The excerpt itemizes the items to be taxed, indicates the amount to be charged for each item, and explains who will control the money the taxes yield and what that money will be spent on. An assignment and an ensuing class discussion ask students to review this information and to then proceed to a discussion of whether or not the Stamp Act was a fair measure. They are also asked to recall what they have learned about colonial income levels and to speculate on how different colonial socio-economic groups might have responded to the Stamp Act. Starting the unit with a primary source document rather than a textbook account in this instance allows students to contribute hypotheses that place their thinking at center stage.

Pedagogical Concerns

In shaping this assignment I try to select additional readings that present varying levels of difficulty. This allows everyone, regardless of reading ability, to familiarize themselves with a basic narrative of events and prepare to argue about that narrative in class. But in an inquiry classroom of differently skilled readers, it also permits students with better comprehension skills to deepen everyone's understanding by introducing evidence from the more demanding text and focusing all readers on the written context of that evidence during the class discussion. Furthermore, the use of ideologically distinct sources enables students to see that historical evidence may be viewed differently depending on one's point of view, thereby demystifying the textbook and giving students additional license to cultivate their own perspective. In this instance, I particularly want them to begin thinking about the relationship of mass and elite forms of protest, which are described differently in the readings.

Multiple Perspectives

Students are now positioned to develop further their analysis of the Stamp Act revolt by examining some contrasting primary source documents that resistance to it produced. The first document they scrutinize is the "Declaration of the Stamp Act Congress," published in October 1765 by a group of colonial assembly leaders meeting in New York City. It is a difficult text for many high school students to read and I take different approaches to dissecting it depending on students' aptitude, motivation, and particular interest. Sometimes I have them "translate" all or parts of the document in small groups, come up with group answers to questions using evidence from the text, and then discuss those questions as an entire class. At other times I read the document aloud and discuss it section by section with the entire class. I am primarily interested in having them assess the authors' attitudes toward the King, Parliament, and England in general as well as their descriptions of the Stamp Act's impact on the colonies.

From my own perspective the Stamp Act Declaration is a complex but relatively moderate document that humbly states the case for colonial autonomy and implores the King to protect the rights of privileged North American colonists as Englishmen. However, I am not interested in imposing this interpretation on the students, although I will push them to debate "translations" that I think are especially mistaken. Recently, for example, one class had a very productive dispute over whether or not this declaration was a Loyalist document. A considerable amount of evidence from the text was thoughtfully presented and critiqued by both sides before I decided to inform them that one was right. My main concern is that any arguments they have about this Declaration's tone or meaning lead them to a deeper understanding of the political and economic tensions that marked colonial relations with England, especially among the elite.

The class then turns to a pair of anonymous letters to colonial newspapers regarding the Stamp Act that describe both its impact and British responsibility in much harsher terms. The letters probably display the perspective of more middle class elements in the colonies. Where the Declaration decries Parliament's decision to tax the colonies as being "inconsistent with the Principles and Spirit of the British Constitution" and labels the duties "extremely Burdensome and Grievous," one letter addresses the British lawmakers as "Ye ruthless crew! Ye infernal, corrupted, detested incendiaries!" and sarcastically urges them to "come see how well we bear additional taxes! See our poor starving! Our liberties expiring! Our trade declining! Our countrymen despairing!" The letters also, like many other written protests of the period, compare the plight of the colonies to "Slavery." Once again, students decode the language and proceed to compare the letters' descriptions with those of the Stamp Act

Congress. This invariably leads to a debate over why they differ and which one paints a more accurate picture of the law's impact and the colonists' resistance. That debate, as well as discussion of what "slavery" meant in this context, begins a reexamination of the issue of popular participation in the Revolution raised at the outset of the course.

The controversy surrounding popular participation and support sharpens as the class then moves to an investigation of the Stamp Act Riots. Students first consider the November 7, 1765 edition of the New York *Gazatte: Post Boy* that describes mob violence against the colonial government officials and institutions on the streets of New York City. They compare the impact and nature of this resistance to the types embodied by the letters and the Stamp Act Declaration. Numerous questions are raised about the rituals connected to the rioting and the question of whether this form of resistance had greater impact than the Stamp Act Declaration is frequently debated.

SECONDARY SOURCES

Now that students have begun to form their own ideas about the politics of Stamp Act resistance, I sometimes introduce two other contrasting secondary source accounts of the event. The first, an excerpt from either Howard Zinn's *A People's History of the United States* or Paul Gilje's *Mobocracy* stresses the rioting, the lower class economic resentments that were part of it, and the worries that upper class resistance leaders had about controlling it. The second, a section of Daniel Boorstin's high school American history textbook (*A History of the United States*), describes colonial resistance as centering on town meetings and merchant non-importation agreements. Boorstin also depicts attacks on Stamp Act tax collectors as the work of "some of the richest and most respectable Americans" who "formed a secret society known as the Sons of Liberty."

The Inquiry Process

Students must now decide which history of the Stamp Act resistance story is more accurate or explain what additional information they would need to make a decision. While they may not be able to pursue that information, just thinking about it gives them a better sense of what it is that historians actually do when they practice their craft: look for evidence to confirm or deny their beliefs about what actually happened in the past, and draw conclusions about the past on the basis of evidence. At the same time, they are grappling with important questions about how change generally occurs and the relationship of the different forces in society that produce change in a particular historical era.

The Boston Massacre

8

Political violence is often an especially compelling indicator of historical change and the story of the Boston Massacre is no exception to this rule. It raises important questions about the development of the American revolutionary process, the nature and social composition of the coalition that supported the Revolution, the relationship of revolutionary leaders to the American people in the streets, the concept of heroism, and the role of propaganda in the Revolution. Moreover, it was and remains an incredibly dramatic and controversial event that clearly demonstrates the way in which political and historical forces and perspectives influence our notion of the truth. It never fails to excite students' passions and it invariably leads them to connect the aspects of the conflict to their own experience.

THE QUARTERING ACT

I open this unit with a brief look at the Quartering Act, which required American colonists to provide food, shelter, and other domestic supplies to the more than 6,000 British troops that were a standing army in the North American colonies in the period leading up to independence. Discussion of a few secondary source descriptions of its provisions and immediate impact prompts questions about the purpose of this army's deployment and the role played by soldiers in colonial society that will be reexamined as the class investigates the "Massacre." The sources also provide information about the legal and legislative conflicts that preceded violent opposition. This, of course, raises once more questions about the efficacy of different forms of resistance and sets the table for yet another discussion of matters such as who led the Revolution and what the relationship was between more elite and more popular action.

SECONDARY SOURCES

At this point, I give students a homework assignment that requires them to read several different secondary source accounts of the Massacre. Again, what I look for when selecting these readings are contrasting interpretations, varying degrees of depth, and different points of emphasis. I also consider the readings' sensitivity to the questions that have been most important to the group I am working with each term. In recent years, however, I have tended to include four particular selections more than others.

The first, a two-paragraph excerpt from a British high school textbook, dispassionately depicts an aggressive colonial mob, describes the event as "this so-called 'Boston Massacre,'" and attributes its impact to "inaccurate" and "inflammatory" propaganda. The second, a somewhat more demanding two-paragraph excerpt from Zinn's *People's History,* views the Massacre as an outgrowth of job competition between soldiers and working class Bostonians and highlights popular participation in the mobilization that followed. A third source is a chapter on the Boston Massacre from Joy Hakim's highly popular junior high text, *A History of US*. Hakim's book, while recognizing the importance of the event, labels Crispus Attucks and the other Massacre victims "troublemakers," argues that they cannot be considered heroes and, instead, grants that status to John Adams who, despite his opposition to the Quartering Act, defended the British soldiers against charges of manslaughter. I typically follow Hakim with an explicitly different perspective, that of Kareem Abdul-Jabbar, who maintains that Attucks was indeed a hero who provided an inspiring example of resistance and embodied an important link between the struggle for independence and the struggle against chattel slavery.

As they go through the sources, students are required to highlight or underline information that helps them to answer some or all of the following questions:

1. Who or what was responsible for the Boston Massacre?
2. What were Crispus Attucks and the "mob" of colonists at the Boston Massacre fighting for?
3. What was Attucks and the "mob's" relationship to leaders such as Sam Adams, Paul Revere, and the Sons of Liberty?
4. Should Crispus Attucks and the other men who died at the Boston Massacre be seen as heroes of the American Revolution?
5. How did the Boston Massacre push the thirteen colonies further along the road to Revolution?

Other questions may be added or substituted depending on the issues that emerge in the exchanges preceding the assignment.

In the discussion that follows, students debate these questions and are strongly encouraged to use and respond to evidence from the readings as they do so. Attucks and the "mob" are regularly praised, exalted, belittled, or completely rebuked by different sections of the class and the issue of responsibility is hotly debated as well. The African-American role in the Revolution and African-American responses to it also become a focus. Each of these arguments raises further questions that can then be pursued through a wide variety of primary sources on the Massacre or digressions into other important aspects of the Revolution.

If, for example, students want to know about the soldiers' prior relations with the community or more about how the confrontation that led to the killing began or what Attucks's role was, the class can turn to two or three conflicting contemporary descriptions of the incident. My current preferences are a selection from a pamphlet written by three prominent Bostonians sympathetic to the American cause, an excerpt from a letter written by the commander of British forces in North America to one of the King's leading ministers, and John Adams's courtroom summation in defense of the accused British soldiers. I also take a separate look at different versions of Paul Revere's engraving depicting the Massacre and some other visual depictions as well. The documents are scrutinized for details relating to these issues and discussion hinges on why students are persuaded or not by the claims those details seem to make. Because some of these texts are more challenging, I usually have kids work on them in class, which means having them read, interpret, and argue over smaller sections of "evidence" in a more incremental fashion.

The Inquiry Process

Conducting discussions that encourage students to exchange viewpoints, deploy evidence, and respond critically to arguments and evidence requires the use of a variety of inquiry techniques. I come to class with a list of potential discussion questions, some of which come directly from the assignment and others which occur to me as I review and prepare the material. My list of questions is always far greater than the number of questions that actually get discussed. When I pose a question, I listen carefully for disagreements and differences in the students' responses. I keep a written record of what they have said and occasionally rearticulate their differences and ask them to respond once more (e.g., "Matt and Jazmin are saying that there is no evidence that Attucks and the mob favored independence, so how can they be considered heroes of the Revolution? Carmen agrees and says that drunks can't be heroes. Ian, on the other hand, is saying that since the fight against the Quartering Act led to the Revolution and changed people's thinking, this makes Attucks and the others heroes. And Jennifer says that, according to an earlier reading, no one in the colonies was thinking about full independence at this time and wants to know does that mean even Washington and Jefferson were not heroes of the Revolution until 1776? What do people think? Are Matt, Jazmin, and Carmen right or are Ian and Jennifer?")

While there are questions that I think are particularly important, I tend to let those that spark student interest have a dominant place in the discussion. This does not mean indulging irrelevant concerns, but it does require connecting digressive questions back to larger ones. For example, a discussion of rank and file heroism in 1770 may elicit a comparison to the role of police and firemen in the events surrounding 9/11. This in turn may lead to a debate over whether action taken in the "War on Terror" can be compared to street brawls with British soldiers. Or, there may be prolonged argument over whether or not Boston's unemployed had other, non-violent means of redressing their grievances. When this happens it is periodically important for me to summarize the different viewpoints paying special attention to disputed evidence, remind students of the road map that led them to these disputes, and restate the original questions (e.g., What were Attucks and the "mob" fighting for? Should they be seen as heroes of the Revolution?) This scaffolding of their ideas helps them to clarify, develop, and organize their thinking and mirrors what I want them to do when I ask them to read and write. It also helps me to organize the exchanges, making decisions about when to move on to a new question, when and how to link the questions that are on the floor, when to press for more evidence, when to introduce or ignore evidence that has been overlooked, when to rule a comment inappropriate or irrelevant, and which of the disputed questions and issues requiring further research should be included in a concluding summary of the entire discussion.

The amount of time we spend on the Boston Massacre varies. If there is tremendous curiosity and analysis being brought to bear on a particular issue, I will pursue it at the cost of addressing other planned topics. If John Adams's description of Crispus Attucks as a "stout Molatto fellow, whose very looks, was enough to terrify any person" is deemed an appeal to racism, raising anew the question of African-American responses to the Revolution, I may decide to have the class examine additional sources that shed light on this. These might include concurrent African-American petitions demanding equal rights and the abolition of slavery or a modern historian's description of black colonial life in New England. If I choose to do so, it is incumbent on me to reconnect this investigation to the larger themes of the course, such as the causes of the Revolution, how it unfolded, and whose interest it represented or not.

The Golden Hill Riots

After analyzing these matters in a Bostonian context, I usually examine them in a New York City setting via an exploration of the Golden Hill Riots, a street brawl between soldiers and patriots that preceded the Boston Massacre by six weeks. This allows students to grasp the broader character of the colonists' clashes with the British military. It also literally affords them the opportunity to view the struggle on their own turf in New York City, sparking their imaginations and enlivening documents and texts in a way that connects history to daily life and to the world that more immediately surrounds them.

PRIMARY AND SECONDARY SOURCES

There are a number of different secondary source descriptions of the Golden Hill Riots that can be used to introduce this topic. I prefer a six-page excerpt from Ralph Ketchum's *Divided Loyalties: How the American Revolution Came to New York*, which is dramatic, accessible, and limited to a description of the events comprising and surrounding the riot itself. Students are asked to read Ketchum, list what they think were the most important events that led to the rioting, identify who or what they think was responsible for the rioting, and then explain their choices in writing using evidence from the reading.

The ensuing class discussion focuses on these issues as well as a comparison of Golden Hill to the Boston Massacre. Once again, additional questions are raised, setting the stage for a look at relevant primary sources. My favorites are a pair of broadsides that were directly involved in the violence. The first, written by a leading New York Son of Liberty, bemoans the social and economic impact that British soldiers have had on New York City and describes a series of violent incidents surrounding those soldiers' attempts to destroy a colonial Liberty Pole. The second, written by British soldiers in direct response to the first, paints a very different picture of the soldiers in New York and describes the same series of incidents from a very different perspective. The contrast is striking and once students have carefully perused the documents with my assistance, their discussion of which is more accurate about the conflict between soldiers and colonists is typically very animated and analytical. Parallels with police and minority groups in contemporary America are argued for, class tensions within colonial New York are detected, and numerous questions are raised about many of the conflicting details. If interest in the episode is high, other written and visual documents are pursued, allowing students to act as historians, piecing together the truth as they see it. Sometimes, they examine another secondary source that quotes or references the documents they have seen and decide whether or not they think the writer's interpretation of them is accurate.

MAPPING AND WALKING TOUR

The unit concludes with a walking tour of lower Manhattan that visits the site of the rioting and other important colonial and Revolutionary landmarks and familiarizes students with social and geographic boundaries of New York in the late eighteenth century. In preparation for the tour I ask students to use their historical imaginations and draw maps of New York City circa 1770 on large pieces of blank paper. I ask that these maps include streets, important buildings and key locations. I then group students, have group members compare their maps, and draw group maps that they agree upon. As each group presents their map to the full class, numerous questions are raised about the city's geography in the revolutionary era. We begin to answer those questions by comparing their maps to copies of a wonderfully detailed late eighteenth century street map of New York (from Burrows and Wallace's *Gotham*) that denotes churches, taverns, government buildings, and more. The *Gotham* map raises further questions about a host of social, economic, racial, and political relationships in the city. If time and logistics permit it, local historians are invited to the classroom to answer some of them.

Finally, students are given current New York City street maps. They place these alongside the *Gotham* maps and are given an excerpt from a lengthy historical article on the Golden Hill Riots that describes their geographical trajectory ("Lobster Backs, Liberty Boys, and Laborers in the Streets: New York's Golden Hill and Nassau Street Riots," by Lee R. Boyer). In small groups or as a full class they connect the excerpt's account to both maps and plan the route through the streets they will take during the part of the walking tour that covers the riots. The planning is an enjoyable but challenging task, partly because many students have never walked through the Wall Street area of Lower Manhattan where much of the action took place and also because they must reconcile the changes that have occurred in the last two hundred years. This requires them to resolve differences they may have about precisely where things occurred in 1770 and where those places are on the map today.

The Tour

The tour itself begins at the recently discovered African burial ground just north of Chambers Street, which was the barricaded northern border of the city in the 1770s. (As, the *Gotham* map indicates, African and Jewish Americans had their own separate burial grounds outside the borders of the city.) At the first site I provide each student with a packet of eighteenth century visual images gleaned from a New York Historical Society collection and copies of some of the documents we've examined in class. I speak briefly about the site and about African Americans in eighteenth century New York, referring them to relevant images and information in their packets, and answering any questions they have. On some tours I ask them to take notes or to write down what they thought was most interesting about the site or how they imagined it looked more than two hundred years ago or what they think about the way it is presented to the public today. The notes and comments become the basis of our next class discussion. Students usually give them to me for safekeeping and sometimes I type them up for the entire class to read before the discussion begins. This procedure is repeated at each of the sites.

We then proceed south to City Hall Park, which in colonial times was "the Common," a locus of public and political gatherings. The Common was where the 1765 Stamp Act Riots began and where the Declaration of Independence was first read in the city in 1776. It was also home to the soldiers' barracks, the city jail, and several Liberty Poles erected by protesting colonists. Across the street on Broadway was a tavern, which was the site of a brawl between colonists and soldiers that led to rioting on Golden Hill. The precise location of these places is etched in writing on the concrete park walk surface along with other historical information. There is also a metal replica of a Liberty Pole next to the modern City Hall.

Next, the tour walks down Broadway stopping at St. Paul's and Trinity Churches, both of which figured significantly in the revolutionary and post-revolutionary periods. St. Paul's was the Church of the American patriotic leaders (George Washington's separate pew remains there today), while Trinity was a hotbed of Tory sentiment. Stops at these sites bring the role of elites and the Revolutionary War in New York City into the picture. The gravestones in Trinity alone constitute a complex and interesting social history of the city. We also pause on western Wall Street, near the Stock Exchanges, where Zenger's Journal was published and where Washington took his first oath of office.

At the bottom of Broadway the tour stops at Bowling, the site of the Customs House, Fort Greene, and numerous assaults on property during the Stamp Act Riots. In 1776, colonists marched here from the Common and pulled down a statue of King George, which was then converted to bullets and cannonballs. Nearby is Fraunces Tavern, a hotbed of patriotic activity in the 1760s and 70s and the place where Washington gave a farewell speech to his officers and the end of the war. The Tavern is both a museum and national landmark, containing a wide variety of revolutionary and colonial artifacts, preserved interiors, and a staff that is eager to work with educators. Because it adds so much to the students' sense of what eighteenth century life was like, Fraunces Tavern requires substantial time and frequently concludes a day's worth of touring.

Moving from Fraunces Tavern northeast to the intersection of Water and Wall Streets, the tour reaches the site of New York's riverside Slave Market, whose images are included in the students' packets. Not coincidentally, this intersection was also the location of the Tontine Coffee House, where merchants created New York's first stock exchange. It is of particular interest to the tour because it is probably where the Sons of Liberty broadside that precipitated the Golden Hill riots (and read in class by the students) was posted on a cold January morning in 1770. If possible, we try at this point to reread some of this document, review Boyer's historical description, and, ignoring the office towers that surround us, try to imagine the confrontation between soldiers and patriots that happened here over two hundred years ago. Literally and figuratively, we follow a mob of Americans and a group of soldiers up Water Street to John Street, turning left onto John and up the small, eastern rise of the street that was Golden Hill (named for the golden wheat fields that were there). Here we imagine the column of British soldiers that joined their comrades and the growing mob that taunted them as they walked up the hill and back toward their barracks on the Common. All along John going west to Nassau Street soldiers and colonists fought each other using swords, sticks, stones, and their fists. As the class retraces this route, we talk once more about the impact the rioting had on a city of roughly 30,000 people. This discussion concludes the walking tour.

10   The Boston Tea Party

The Boston Tea Party is usually the next focus of attention. Consequently, unless there is considerable student interest, the Townshend Acts and colonial non-importation agreements that preceded the Intolerable Acts are not explored in depth. Some historians have argued persuasively that these consumer boycotts were not only a pivotal element in the popular revolutionary mobilization, but also the foundation of an American political identity. My decision to pay less attention to them does not reflect disagreement with this view. It is rather the result of the dilemmas I face as an inquiry teacher. First, I have not yet organized a compelling enough combination of documents, secondary readings, and activities in this area to make it accessible to students. Second, and perhaps most importantly, at this point in the class I often feel the need to move toward some sort of chronological completion. Because I want students to make broader assessments of the Revolution, I do think they need some familiarity with its overall trajectory and terrain and I worry about getting bogged down in particulars, no matter how enriching or significant they may be. While rejecting the traditional push through a superficial timeline, I still feel compelled to "finish" at least the broad strokes of the narrative that constitute the framework of the course. Therefore, I make choices, engaging in a struggle between depth and coverage that is central to the inquiry approach. In any event, the boycott issue is indeed part of the Tea Party story, the next point of investigation.

The Tea Party draws interest partly because it occupies a central place in our national, historical memory of the Revolution. However, a closer look at it sheds considerable light on many of the course's essential questions such as what caused the American Revolution, who supported and opposed it, what was the relationship between the Revolution's "leaders" and the people in the streets, and how did popular consciousness shift from reform to independence and revolution?

I find the best way to enter these questions is to have students read two or three contrasting textbook accounts of the Tea Party and then attempt to reconstruct and interpret it. The texts I use most frequently are again chosen for difference in viewpoint, style, and depth. The excerpt from Robert Sobel's *The American Revolution,* is a substantial but easy read that provides an extremely thorough explanation of the political and economic context in which the Tea Act and resistance to it occurred. Sobel pays particular attention to Boston tea smugglers, their connection to the Sons of Liberty, and the difficulty they had mobilizing popular support prior to the Tea Party. Gary Nash offers a more concise and demanding treatment that stresses the Sons' role as a unifier of public sentiment. Howard Zinn, on the other hand, argues that the Sons looked to restrain class antagonisms and attacks on property in the protests that occurred when England responded to the Tea Party with the Coercive Acts. Edmund Morgan highlights the competing interests of colonial merchants and the East India Company and, like Nash, depicts a smooth and direct link between the Sons and the colonists in general.

Questioning and Discussion

The written homework questions attached to these readings simply ask students to provide one or two sentence answers to the following questions:

1. Why did the British Parliament think that most Americans would favor the Tea Act? In other words, why did England think this law would make life easier for most American colonists?

2. Which particular group of colonists was most opposed to the Tea Act and why?

3. What exactly was the Boston Tea Party?

4. What laws did the British Parliament pass in response to the Tea Party and what did those laws do?

5. How did people in the thirteen British colonies respond to the laws mentioned in the previous question?

The discussion that follows this assignment begins with a review of these questions, but in most cases quickly proceeds to an analysis of the stake that different social classes had in the Tea Party and the role played by the Sons in fomenting rebellion. Some students, focusing on savings to the American consumer, see the Sons as middle class manipulators who provoked repression to garner working class support. Others, noting the thousands of Tea Party witnesses, regard them as leaders whose actions dramatized the entire nation's interest.

Writing Assignment

I take careful notes on this debate, photocopy them, and give each student a copy. I then ask them to write an essay for homework on whether the Sons and their tea merchant allies sincerely led or crassly manipulated the colonial masses, using evidence from the notes and readings to support their viewpoint and critique opposing ones. The essay question itself is phrased differently each time I conduct this exercise, depending on the language and focus of the class discussion.

The only primary source document I use in this unit is the "Resolutions of the New York Sons of Liberty," which condemned the Tea Act and called for a total boycott of imported tea. The resolutions circulated widely in New York, helping to prompt a New York Tea Party that quickly followed the Boston one. I usually read the document aloud in class, asking students to comment on what they think it reveals about the Sons, their motives, and their relationship to "the people." This gives us an opportunity to closely examine and evaluate the various appeals and arguments the document makes. Particularly striking to most students are the repeated comparisons of the colonists' predicament to slavery (e.g., "the execution of that Act, involves our slavery, and would sap the foundation of our freedom, whereby we should become slaves to our brethren and our fellow subjects. . ."").

These references, which appear in many other writings of the period, not only raise questions about the Sons' intentions, but also reconnect the class back to concerns about the Revolution's attitude toward slavery and African Americans raised at the outset of the course. If discussion of the latter is especially animated, I am once more confronted with the problem of whether to delve more deeply into a point of strong interest or to revisit the matter when the Revolution's basic chronology has been covered. In any case, I remind students that more complete answers to any of the questions argued in this discussion would require us to view and analyze additional documents and assorted evidence connected to the event.

The Tea Party readings contain various descriptions of the colonial response to the Coercive Acts, including the formation of the First Continental Congress. This, of course, leaves the class on the doorstep of armed conflict and the Declaration of Independence. After reading the Declaration's grievances against the Crown, which now appear far more comprehensible, the students debate their contemporary relevance. I facilitate this by having them sort the grievances, individually and in small groups, into those that America today has resolved and those that might still be lodged against the present government. If time permits, we may examine and assess some historical and modern-day adaptations of the Declaration (e.g., Seneca Falls, the National Labor Union, Ian Watson's recent *Declaration of Independence from President George II*).

The military conduct of the Revolution is a rich, engaging subject that sheds further light on the race, class, and resistance issues that have already been explored. It also raises new concerns: the role of Washington, the friction over paper money that reorganized the revolutionary coalition and presaged the postwar Shays' Rebellion, and the status of women. Rather than explore these matters directly in this setting, I prefer to confine our coverage of the war itself to an in-class lecture, which can occupy up to two class sessions depending on the number of questions students ask. Using a few maps and illustrations, the lecture essentially tells the chronological story of the trials, tribulations, and eventual triumph of the American armed forces in the years 1775-1781. At the outset, I make it clear that the "facts" I am presenting are nonetheless couched in judgments that are my own (e.g., that French aid was crucial to the American victory). Sometimes I even have students review their lecture notes and distinctly highlight items that are fact and opinion. My primary purpose, however, is to convey the nature of the conflict, the strategy employed by both sides, the manner of American victory, and the reasons for it. However, there is a significant drama in much of the story that I like to convey as well. The Battle of New York, for example, was a frightening, rapid rout that taught Washington important tactical lessons and covered easily identifiable terrain in three of the city's current boroughs. Many students find the lecture compelling, perhaps because of the depth of knowledge they already bring to the topic and the freedom they have to ask (and research) questions that occur to them.

11 George Washington

After a brief examination of the war's settlement and England's recognition of American independence, the course moves into an extensive exploration of the question, Who were the "Founding Fathers"?

A focus on Washington flows logically from our review of the Revolutionary War.

SECONDARY SOURCES

Following the pattern established in the examinations of the Boston Massacre and the Tea Party, I assign students a packet of secondary source assessments of Washington's military and political leadership and his attitude toward slavery and African Americans during the war. The packet's first part typically includes an older high school textbook's sanitized account of him as heroic in every respect, Zinn's description of a harsh disciplinarian who ultimately sided with Congress when his underpaid soldiers challenged it, conservative historian Richard Brookhiser's portrait of an inspiring guerilla warrior who, though not a military genius, created conditions that were essential for victory, and an Englishman's more measured judgment that balances Washington's resilience, valor, and dignity with his inability to win a clear-cut, unassisted victory on the battlefield. The second part offers varying takes on Washington's changing attitude toward the presence of black soldiers in his army. Here again, Brookhiser's work is set alongside that of African-American historian Benjamin Quarles or a selection from either Eli Ginzburg and Alfred Eichner's *The Troublesome Presence* or Henry Wiencek's more recent *An Imperfect God.*

WRITING ASSIGNMENT The homework asks students to highlight and label evidence that casts Washington in a particularly positive or negative light and to be prepared to use that evidence in a discussion of how we should judge the role he played in the Revolution. If the discussion centers on his military actions there are other primary and secondary sources that can be used to inform any disputes that arise. However, the issue of slavery and black military participation usually receives greater attention. If that is the case, I like to work with an eleven-page section of an outstanding collection of Washington's letters, proclamations, memos, and legal documents compiled by a National Center for History in the Schools team. The section documents his evolving and sometimes contradictory views on slavery, prejudice, and African Americans in general. The items range from a 1766 note arranging the sale of one of his slaves to the West Indies, to one that explains his decision in 1779 to stop selling his slaves, to his last will and testament which freed his slaves upon his death. They are usually read aloud in class (though this need not be the case) and each item generally generates a great deal of interest and often multiple interpretations. There are frequent disagreements over the meanings of his statements, the validity of his arguments, and the extent to which he should or should not be credited for changes in his attitudes.

In this context, it is sometimes helpful to reexamine Brookhiser, Quarles, Ginzburg, and Wieneck to see how they quote these documents in developing their arguments and what historical contexts they place them in. It is also useful to examine the poem and letter extolling the Revolution's virtues sent to him by Phyllis Wheatley, an African American slave, an earlier public letter Wheatley wrote condemning slavery, and Washington's reply to Wheatley complimenting her poem and literary skills. Whatever direction it takes, I often conclude this discussion by summarizing the key disputes and assigning an essay on one of them, making sure to stress the use of evidence to support one's position and a thorough response to opposing views.

If the demand is articulated at this point, I sometimes assign a reading on Washington's response to the various groups of women that served, formally or informally, in his army. Ordinarily part of a unit on women and the Revolution offered later in the course, the reading is an excerpt from Ray Raphael's *A People's History of the American Revolution*. It describes the role played by "camp followers," prostitutes, spies, messengers, and undercover soldiers and generously quotes both Washington's relevant orders and letters as well as the private journals of numerous women. Allowing students to assess these women and the general's attitude toward them, enables students to view his role and the general character of the Revolution from a different angle. It also tends to challenge stereotypic assumptions they may have about a presumably excluded group. For example, they are very often surprised that poor women such as Margaret Corbin were actually awarded pensions for service in combat or that others "carried messages, moving freely through a countryside sometimes dominated by the enemy." In general, this digression broadens their grasp of the immediate question (Washington's role) and raises new ones about both women and behavior within the ranks. (For more discussion of the role women played in the Revolutionary War, see Chapter 15).

12 Thomas Jefferson

Thomas Jefferson represents a different dimension of revolutionary leadership more closely associated with ideas, legacies, and ideology. It therefore seems appropriate that an evaluation of him begin with a selection of primary sources. However, it is important that students understand these sources in the context of Jefferson's political career, which began in real estate law and culminated in the Presidency. Before distributing an assignment that contains his thoughts on a wide variety of social, economic, and political subjects, I have students read a short biography of Jefferson that highlights his revolutionary and post-revolutionary occupations and activities.

PRIMARY SOURCES

After a discussion in which they exchange preliminary views of his role and contributions and compare him to Washington, they are given a two-part packet of his writing that may be read either at home or in class. The first part presents in order separate extracts from his writings on wealth and poverty, education, domestic rebellion, individual rights in a democracy, voting qualifications, religion, and slavery. The second is one-page summary of his famous *Notes on the State of Virginia* and a more extensive six-page excerpt from that text, in which he articulates extensively his view of slavery, racial difference, African Americans' abilities, and the future of race relations in the United States.

Students are instructed to read the packet, often in separate sections, and to try to get a clear sense of a) Jefferson's opinions on these issues, b) what they think of his opinions, and occasionally c) what, if anything, those opinions tell them about why the American Revolution occurred and who supported it.

Discussion

Jefferson's ideas tend to generate substantial responses and their analysis often requires a considerable amount of time. Reading the first parts of the packet, students are generally struck by his radicalism, which not a few of them find surprising and in certain instances objectionable. There is frequent disagreement, for example, over his notion that government has an obligation to provide farmers who have lost their land with employment. On the other hand, there is usually praise for his prophetic advocacy of mass public education and full university scholarships for qualified but needy students. His condemnation of slavery, his perceptive description of the damage it does to both master and slave, and his indictment of freedom-seeking slave owners are equally commended but invariably raise questions of how Jefferson reconciled these views with his life-long ownership of slaves.

Few discussions of those questions prepare them for the complex but transparent racism that pervades *Notes on Virgina*. Jefferson's ample descriptions of blacks as intellectually inferior, morally primitive, and sexually licentious raise many hackles, but they inevitably prompt some to claim that Jefferson, as a product of his time and of limited experience with free and educated black people, cannot be faulted for these beliefs. This debate takes us in and out of the text as I press students for evidence to support their views. If the demand for additional evidence regarding Jefferson's contact with African Americans is strong, I frequently turn to his correspondence with Benjamin Banneker, a black mathematician, inventor, astronomer, surveyor, and abolitionist as well as documents connected to his relationship with Sally Hemmings.

JEFFERSON AND BENJAMIN BANNEKER

The correspondence with Banneker, written ten years after *Notes on Virginia*, is fascinating for several reasons. First, it is clear that Banneker is highly educated, articulate, and at pains to discredit ideas about black inferiority and enlist Jefferson's support for both his work and abolitionist efforts. Second, one is struck by Jefferson's now very different analysis of black deficiencies. ("Nobody wishes more than I do to see such proofs, as you exhibit, that nature has given to our black brethren talents equal to those of the other colours of men, and that the appearance of a want of them is owing only to the degraded condition of their existence both in Africa and America.") Perhaps the most compelling of the many questions raised by the letters, is whether or not Jefferson had a sincere change of heart in the wake of Banneker's brilliance or in the ten years that had passed since his previous public musings on race. A third letter, written by Jefferson to a white contemporary on the subject of Banneker's requests, while ambiguous, casts doubt on his sincerity. Once again, however, students are divided on the evidence, affording them yet another opportunity to think about how history is researched and written.

JEFFERSON AND SALLY HEMMINGS

A Hemmings/Jefferson packet adds greater scope to our evaluation of Jefferson. It begins with either a *New York Times* article or a page from Roger Wilkins's *Jefferson's Pillow* that precisely delineates recent DNA discoveries connecting Jefferson to his female slave. This summary is paired with the testament of Madison Hemmings, which claims Hemmings and Jefferson as parents, describes the history of their liaison, and recalls Jefferson's plantation relationship with the four slave children Madison says he had with Hemmings. These documents predictably inspire a host of controversial questions. These tend to include: Did the relationship with Hemmings in fact occur? How should we judge Jefferson's relationship with Sally and her children if Madison's claims are true? Is Jefferson equally culpable if his nephew fathered Sally's children under his watch? Are Jefferson's possible personal and sexual relations with a female slave relevant to a consideration of his ideas, achievements, and overall impact, and what, if anything, does the Hemmings affair tell about the American Revolution and slavery? Students are generally quite capable of discussing these matters in a serious, thoughtful manner and of connecting them to the larger issues of the Revolution, with some prompting and direction on my part. Having digested and analyzed several primary sources, they are now ready to test their own evaluations against those of professional historians and journalists.

SECONDARY SOURCES

I now give them a packet containing opposing secondary source treatments of Jefferson, most of which reference at least one of the primary sources they have considered. In the packet I try to combine highly accessible and more challenging pieces that alternately laud or condemn him or seek a middle ground. I tend to place the less demanding reads first to insure that at least part of the packet is commonly read and understood. As I've already indicated, students who advance to and digest the more comprehensive texts can then contribute arguments and evidence from them in a manner that makes sense to everyone.

The packet usually begins with portions of a sixty-year-old pamphlet written by Jefferson biographer Claude Bowers that hails his many contributions. Bowers attempts to reconcile what he regards as Jefferson's abolitionist activism with his status as a slave owner, arguing that emancipating his own slaves would have been a meaningless, ineffectual act on Jefferson's part. The Bowers piece is followed by a lengthy but easily read editorial from a now defunct black magazine of the 1990's entitled *Founding Slaveowners.* The editorial contrasts the Declaration's rhetoric about equality with *Notes on Virginia*'s explicit racism and denounces all efforts to portray him and other "so-called founding fathers" as freedom fighters. The next selection is a chapter on Jefferson from Joy Hakim's aforementioned *A History of US,* which depicts Jefferson as the father of human rights in general, draws attention to his impact on education and religious liberty in America, and leaves unmentioned his views on race and slavery.

A very different view from Hakim's is contained in a *Washington Post* article that surveys several different viewpoints at a conference on "Jeffersonian Legacies," but devotes most of its ink to Paul Finkelman, a historian who views Jefferson primarily as a self-indulgent racist. Rounding out the required readings is a short, highly nuanced, but ultimately sympathetic *New York Times* op-ed piece by Harvard sociologist Orlando Patterson entitled "Jefferson the Contradiction." Patterson acknowledges Jefferson's racism, but argues that it "must be understood in the context of his times and his relationship with an African-American woman." He also maintains that the longevity of Jefferson's relationship with Sally Hemmings "humanizes" him and "suggests that his doubts about his racialist theories may have been more serious than he let on in his writings."

Finally, as a supplement for more skilled or ambitious readers, I attach a combination of more detailed and complex readings by historians such as Gary Wills, Roger Wilkins, Arthur Schlesinger, Jr., Pauline Maier and Gary Nash. These selections analyze Jefferson in the context of the Alien and Sedition Acts, the electoral college, the Haitian Revolution, the Northwest Ordinance, and other events beyond the scope of the Revolution. Needless to say, the packet provides new evidence that confirms or denies views already articulated and introduces new and provocative arguments that the students have never considered. It is not possible for them to digest and analyze all of this with each other, but my job is to focus them on the arguments they find most interesting and to push their evaluation of them to a higher level.

Having explored the role of our official founders, the class now turns to the actions and ideas of African Americans, Native Americans, women, and the working classes, reexamining their roles in the Revolution, assessing its impact on their lives, and measuring the influence these apparently subordinate people had on the nation's enduring character and traditions. A wide variety of provocative primary and secondary sources are available for all of these groups. However, the attention given each varies depending on student interest and the time remaining in the course. At the very least, I aim to raise important questions about each group and whet students' appetites to the extent that some may elect to do further research on one of them when they write a final paper.

13 African Americans and the American Revolution

I like to begin this section of the course with African Americans partly because their presence in the Jefferson story inevitably raises questions about their larger presence in the colonies and their response to the Revolution. However, years of examining documents from the revolutionary era have also convinced me that what John Brown called "this Negro question" was central to the way in which American revolutionaries defined themselves and to the entire revolutionary process. The innumerable references condemning England's attempt to reduce the colonies to "slavery" that appear in the letters, petitions, newspaper articles, and broadsides of the period were not idle, trifling or exaggerated metaphors. In fact, many revolutionary leaders repeatedly described their oppression at the hands of England in explicitly racial terms, as the following statements make clear:

> [If] an impartial and independent administration of justice is once wrested from your hands. . . you will become slaves indeed, in no respect different from the sooty Africans, whose persons and properties are subject to the disposal of their tyrannical masters.
>
> (JOSEPH GALLOWAY, 1760)

> They will make Negroes of us all.
>
> (ROBERT LIVINGSTON, 1765)

We won't be their Negroes. Providence never designed us for Negroes. . . and therefore never intended us for slaves.

(JOHN ADAMS, 1765)

You think most if not all the Colonies are Negroes and mulattos—you are wretchedly mistaken—ninety nine in a hundred in the more northern Colonies are white, and there is as great blood flowing in their veins, save the royal blood, as any in the three kingdoms.

(JAMES OTIS, 1765)

The Crisis is arrived when we must assert our Rights, or Submit to every imposition that can be heap'd upon us; till custom and use, will make us tame, and abject slaves, as the Blacks we rule over with such arbitrary sway.

(GEORGE WASHINGTON, 1774)

In these men's eyes, freedom or liberty was closely connected to the right to one's property. Attempts to deny or remove that right, through unjust taxation or any other means, were regarded as steps in the direction of slavery. Moreover, the struggle against England's "enslavement" of the colonies made those who resisted increasingly aware of the denial of rights to African Americans, slave or free. Therefore, an examination of the African American presence in the Revolution is in many respects an inquiry into its essential nature.

QUESTIONING AND DISCUSSION

A few questions have generated the best inquiry into the African American revolutionary experience: What were African Americans' attitudes toward the revolution? What, if anything did they expect from it? How central or marginal was the African American contribution to the revolution?, and Was the Revolution a step forward or backward for African Americans? Again, a wide variety of materials lend themselves quite well to these concerns. Herbert Apthekar's exceptional collection of documents written by African Americans in Massachusetts during the revolutionary period contains several general slave petitions for freedom, legal requests for freedom made by blacks who had served in the Continental Army, formal protests by free blacks against taxation without representation in the revolutionary state government, and demands for African American public education. While often requiring a patient, in-class reading, these historical records are a wonderful window into eighteenth century African-American life and thought. They also reveal the link and tension between the aspirations of blacks and the strivings of the country as a whole.

The questions that I distribute to focus students' examination are designed to raise these issues:

1. What, if anything, does the document tell you about what African Americans wanted or expected from the Revolution?
2. What, if anything, does the document tell you about the connection or the tension between the fight for American independence and the fight against slavery?
3. What, if anything, does the document tell you about African American life and/or race relations at the time of the Revolution?

Needless to say, there are many other primary sources that convey African Americans' relationship to the Revolution, which may or may not be pursued, depending on the questions this set of documents raises and the amount of time available at this point in the course. In any event, as I shift into secondary sources that focus on black participation in the Revolutionary War, I like to combine the more general questions the unit addresses with specific questions that the primary sources have produced.

Recently, for example, I gave students a packet of readings that began with a highly detailed but accessible chronology of black life in the revolutionary era from 1774–1783, proceeded to an excerpt from John Hope Franklin's *From Slavery to Freedom,* and concluded with an optional selection from Apthekar's *The Negro in the American Revolution.* In a previous semester I had merely asked students to highlight information that, in their view, explained what African Americans wanted or expected during the revolutionary period. This time, however, discussion of the primary sources raised two compelling additional questions that I added to the packet's cover sheet:

1. Were African American slaves in the South aware of the Declaration of Independence during the American Revolution?

2. Could slavery have been outlawed throughout the United States after victory in the Revolution?

Of course, there was considerable debate over evidence connected to these questions in the subsequent class discussion. Because interest was so high, I then introduced selections from Gary Nash's *Race and Revolution* which argues that nation-wide abolition was, in fact, a seriously considered possibility in the post-revolutionary moment. Reading much of Nash out loud to the students, I challenged them to respond to each of his major arguments and pieces of evidence. Finally, I asked everyone to write a short essay on whether or not the revolution was a step forward for African Americans, using evidence from all of the readings.

Activity

I sometimes conclude this unit by having students examine and evaluate the portions of several contemporary high school American history textbooks that cover blacks in the Revolution. This allows them to use their newly-found knowledge and opinions to critique these texts and, in the process, reflect on the impact that choices about what to include in school books have on the young people who read them. Students are asked to read the sources, write down brief comments on each one's strengths and weaknesses, and, finally, to identify the "best" and "worst" sources. In class, they present their choices, respond to disagreements, and debate larger questions that are raised. If I am feeling particularly ambitious, I ask small groups to draw up an outline of what their own sections on the subject in a textbook might include.

14

Native Americans and the Revolution

The materials I have garnered on Native Americans and the Revolution are not as extensive, partly because more popular and accessible texts on the Revolution tend to ignore its impact on Native Americans. Moreover, much of the best work in this area has been written for a higher level academic audience. However, the sources I do use tend to evoke a very important issue implicit in the entire Native American revolutionary experience: what is the nature of a people's freedom if obtaining it involves the denial of freedom to another group?

One of the problems I face in presenting the materials is assembling a collection that enables students to defend diverse points of view. The primary sources that assume the virtues of conquest and exclusion tend to impress students as transparently prejudiced (the Declaration itself refers to indigenous people as "merciless Indian savages, whose known rule of warfare is an undistinguished destruction of all ages, sexes, and conditions"). In almost everyone's eyes, they are easily demolished by Indian testimony that is generally dignified, poetic, and persuasive. The more conservative or antiseptic textbooks either omit this chapter in Native American history or dispose of it in one or two sentences. Conversely, historians that devote time to it generally indict revolutionary America's policies in the harshest terms.

In this context, the inquiry teacher's job is not to defend the indefensible for the sake of argument, although playing the devil's advocate of an unpopular view can provide students with a useful challenge. Rather, it is to develop open-ended questions that yield productive thinking. For instance, issues such as whether or not American attitudes could have differed or whether the treatment of Indians somehow invalidates the struggle for independence or why there was not more opposition to anti-Indian policies within the Revolution frequently prompt interesting and provocative differences. Also, Gary Nash's *The American People,* while mincing no words with regard to white racism, presents the military questions facing the colonists on their western border in a manner that allows students to debate whether or not the white American response was justified. On the other hand, it is also politically and intellectually healthy for them simply to confront the rigorous, polemical work of Native American historian Ward Churchill who depicts nearly every white American response to Indians as part of a pattern of genocide. In general, viewing the Revolution from an Indian perspective involves analyzing it in a more complex and provocative manner.

15

Women's Role in the American Revolution

Most Americans think that women, like African Americans, played a minimal, inconsequential role in the Revolution. High school textbooks, which in the wake of the late twentieth century women's movement now include mention of women participants, have done little to challenge this assumption. They tend to confine female revolutionists to inserts or digressions that praise and summarize their work, but rarely analyze their presence or set their contributions in a changing social context. Teachers all too frequently follow their lead, rendering revolutionary gender relations, a potentially exciting and controversial topic, as missing-in-action. In fact, the Revolution set an original American precedent for the pattern of liberation and retrenchment that has marked U.S. social and military mobilization throughout the nation's history. My goal in the unit that covers women in this period is to have students test the validity of their assumptions and further contemplate the nature of the Revolution by exploring its impact on this group.

READINGS AND QUESTIONING

They have already been exposed to some of the issues surrounding women's involvement through their examination of the Ray Raphael excerpt on women in Washington's Army (see page 55). Although I have future plans to begin with an examination of eighteenth century domestic and educational artifacts, I currently open by giving students a packet of two secondary source readings that asks them to highlight or underline information that, in their view, answers the following questions:

1. What was life like for different kinds of American women at the time of the Revolution?

2. What kinds of things did women actually do when they participated in the Revolution?

3. What positive or negative effects did the Revolution have upon women's lives?

4. Did American women connect their own struggle for a better life to the colonies' struggle for independence from England?

The first reading is an easily read two-page excerpt from renowned historian Gerda Lerner's *The Woman in American History.* Lerner provides a general introductory overview of the various actions that women took in support of the revolutionary effort. Her piece is complemented by a more extensive, demanding selection from Mary Beth Norton's *Liberty's Daughters,* which focuses on the social, rather than the political, history of women in the revolutionary era in a dramatic fashion that never ceases to fascinate students. To facilitate its reading I have divided the text into the following sections:

The Problem of Rape During Wartime
Slave Women Seeking Freedom
Women on Their Own, Women Demanding Equality
The Role of Women After the Revolution.

Norton provides students with a more intense and immediate sense of the revolutionary upheaval's impact on daily life and discussion of her work raises a host of important new questions, while permitting consideration of older ones from a different vantage point. These have included:

Why does rape occur so frequently in warfare?

What, if anything, is the purpose of wartime rape and is it, under those circumstances any less malicious?

Were flights to freedom that severely endangered an enslaved woman's children justified?

Should African Americans who joined the British be considered Tories, traitors, or Loyalists?

Were blacks who embraced British offers of freedom naïve or foolish?

What, if anything, did black and white women have in common at this time?

Did women who assumed and subsequently relinquished their control over their husbands' farms and businesses during the war make any overall progress?

Why, in the post-war era, were women removed from whatever non-traditional roles they had assumed during the Revolution?

To what extent did women who spoke out for women's rights, speak for other American women and where did these feminist women's ideas come from?

Several of these questions can be pursued in greater depth, depending again on time, interest, and the importance a teacher places on them. I particularly enjoy having students scrutinize a historian's profile of Abigail Adams that includes substantial portions of her "Remember the Ladies" note to her husband John, his bemused reply, and her subsequent complaint to Mercy Warren about his attitudes. These sources, perfunctorily mentioned in the best of the general American history texts, dispel a variety of historical misconceptions about women in the colonial era and shed an interesting light on the widespread upheaval in almost all areas of life that marked the Revolution. They also reveal something of the traditional founders' attitude towards the less franchised members of the revolutionary coalition. Students are often struck by the tone of the exchanges and spend considerable time debating issues such as the seriousness of Abigail's demands, the sarcasm of John's response, and, of course, the extent to which Abigail and Mercy Warren's sentiments were shared by less elite and educated women in America. When time permits and interest is high, I like to turn them to additional secondary sources that weigh in on these questions. This challenges their analyses and allows them to see how professionals use additional historical information to support and explain their interpretations.

The Working Class and the Revolution

Another unit that I try to include in this part of the course is an examination of two different historians' views of working class participation in the Revolution. The role of ordinary Americans and their relationship to the Revolution's middle and upper class leaders is an issue that students have already grappled with in their investigations of the Stamp Act, the Boston Massacre, the Golden Hill Riots and the Boston Tea Party. Now, however, I want them to dissect and respond to a scholarly polemic on this issue that references the entire revolutionary period and presents opposing views of the Revolution's basic character.

Ironically, the most clear-cut debate on class dynamics within the Revolution occurs between radical historians. "New Leftists" such as Howard Zinn and Jesse Lemisch tend to argue that the Revolution's upper class leaders were able to marginalize radical working class action and direct lower class anger against foreign and domestic oppression into a fight for independence on their terms. In a similar vein, Peter Linebaugh and Marcus Rediker more recently maintain that "moderate patriot" leadership, which had always sought to limit the struggle for liberty, staged an American Thermidor that neutralized the Revolution's "militant origins" and "radical momentum" and brought it to a "conservative political conclusion." In contrast, Herbert Apthekar, an "Old Left" Marxist writing in the Popular Front spirit of the 1930s and 40s, maintains that the interests of the American working classes converged with those of the anti-colonial elite and that they were firm, fully informed supporters of independence and the Revolution.

Digesting and comparing these scholars' claims is not always easy for students, but it can be incredibly rewarding. I typically pair Apthekar with one of the New Left historians and offer students edited versions of both historians' work. To help them deconstruct it, I bracket and number several key arguments and pieces of evidence in each of the readings. I then give students a worksheet that lists each of the bracketed items (e.g., Apthekar #1, Report by British customs official; Lemisch # 2, Pennsylvania State Constitution) and asks them to explain in writing why each item does or does not convince them of the historian's overall argument. This work can be done individually or in class with small groups and followed by a full class discussion of the arguments and evidence students find most compelling. If the exchanges are especially strong, I offer students copies of my notes and ask them to use them along with their worksheets and the readings to write a short essay that presents and defends their own point of view on the role of workers and craftsmen in the Revolution.

17   Final Paper and Conclusion

With three or four weeks left in the term I assign a final paper and decrease regular written assignments to give students time to work on it. I give them a list of possible topics and ask them to choose one. Most of these are derived from the units we have covered, which allows students to analyze issues they have already considered and debated and draw on work they have already done. The topics are expressed as open-ended questions, which range from those concerned with specific events to those that address broader issues. If students want to choose their own topic, they must submit a question and have it approved.

A typical topic list includes many of the following questions, whose precise phrasing may differ depending in part on the discussions that mark each semester:

- Were the men who died at the Boston Massacre heroes of the American Revolution?
- How should we judge Revolutionary leaders such as George Washington and Thomas Jefferson?
- Was the American Revolution a step forward or backward for African Americans?
- Was the American Revolution's response to Native Americans justified?
- Did the Sons of Liberty manipulate or develop ordinary Bostonians' response to the Tea Act?

- Did the Revolution's leaders have the same goals as the masses of Americans who participated in it?
- How is the Declaration of Independence relevant or irrelevant to our lives today?
- Was the American Revolution the will of the majority of the people living in the thirteen colonies?
- Did the Loyalists have a case? Was the American Revolution a "mistake"? Could "America" have thrived under continued British rule?
- Did the American Revolution represent progress for American women?
- Was the War for American Independence a "social revolution"? (Howard Zinn vs. Gordon Wood)
- What were the primary causes of the American Revolution?

If older, more ambitious students choose questions such as the last two, which demand additional research and reading, I encourage them to discuss and debate that material with me and with other students who are also examining them.

Students must develop their own extensive, written answer to one of these questions by presenting and analyzing opposing viewpoints on it. They must therefore build on the numerous reading, writing, and discussion exercises stressing the analysis of argument and evidence that they have engaged in throughout the term. To prepare for this task and help them construct their own guide to writing the paper, I ask them to submit a two-part plan. The first part requires them to write out the question they have chosen, write down a very brief response that they "think is the correct answer to the question," and then list two or three important arguments (with supporting pieces of evidence) that bolster their answer. The second part asks them to write down an opposing answer to the question, two or three opposing arguments and pieces of evidence supporting that answer, and an explanation of why each opposing argument and piece of evidence is either wrong or unconvincing. The plan enables students to spell out their papers' basic elements and map out their terrain. Plans can be converted into more extended outlines if students find that helpful.

There are several ways of concluding the course. One requires having students read and critique each other's papers. Another entails having a panel of teachers, professional historians, or history graduate students debate one of the course's larger or more controversial issues and respond to students' questions and comments in the process. It is also fruitful at this point to examine once more the legacy and contemporary use of the American Revolution. Sometimes, to prompt analysis of the course's pedagogy and perhaps reveal to students the amount of information they have absorbed, I give them a "test" that asks them to identify a substantial list of names, terms, and events associated with the Revolution.

Regardless of which path is taken, I always include a final reflection on the course itself. This involves a discussion of matters such as what students feel were the most important things they learned, instances in which things they learned or analyzed in class came up in discussions or encounters beyond the school, and what they would like to know more about. These reflections, which often include a written dimension, allow me to assess the course's impact on each student and invariably shape what I do in subsequent terms.

There are other potential features of this course, which have not been examined in this booklet. Film and video, for example, provide a host of opportunities to view history through a different lens and to examine the politics of historical depictions in the popular culture. Hollywood portraits such as *1776* or *Revolution* starring Al Pacino are particularly entertaining sources of information that students enjoy critiquing. It is also fun and highly instructive for the class as a whole to research controversies that arise in their discussions, heading to the library stacks, the Internet, or a collection of textbooks on a quest for answers. Surveying people in the street about their historical knowledge and viewpoints is another productive, thought-provoking exercise. Each of these activities can be integrated at any particular point in the course.

SAMPLE STUDENT PAPERS

The student papers included here were written to meet the social studies requirement for graduation. Students' work is assessed using criteria that determine whether a paper is considered excellent, good, competent, or in need of revision. These three papers indicate the range of possible responses for successfully meeting the social studies requirement.

TO GIVE, TO TAKE, AND TO BE LIED TO: AMERICAN HISTORY

Before doing the research for this paper, I had never really heard about African Americans being involved in the American Revolution; I had only heard about the white men who won the war for America. However, I have discovered the Revolutionary war really could not have been won without help from the African Americans and I think it's time for people to learn about these other people who helped fight it. The main concern of this paper is the issue of whether African Americans gained anything from their efforts, given that legal equality was not accomplished until many years later. But in order to understand and resolve this issue we first have to understand their situation at the time of American Revolution, what they wanted or expected from the Revolution, what the Revolution promised them, and what exactly they got from it. Only then can we judge the extent to which it benefited them.

Before the Revolutionary war most African Americans were slaves. The few African Americans who were free lived in the Northern states. Slavery was very popular and profitable in America. When Thomas Jefferson wrote the Declaration of Independence, he included a clause condemning the King of Britain for having and permitting slavery and the slave trade. Jefferson wrote, "He has waged cruel war against human nature itself, violating its most sacred rights of life and liberty in the persons of a distant people who never offended him, captivating them and carrying them into slavery in another hemisphere, or to incur miserable death in their transportation thither..."

The clause caused a great disturbance and was removed from the Declaration. This was due to the fact that many citizens of the 13 states were very much for slavery. Many called Jefferson a hypocrite for writing such a piece since he himself had slaves. On the other hand, one might argue he was saying "do as I say not as I do," for perhaps he truly believed that slavery was a horrible thing and he was just a product of his time. As Weisberger (author of The Impact Of Our Past) explains, " . . . people can and do describe a perfect world worth struggling for without being perfect themselves." In any case, Jefferson himself is an example of the contradiction in the American independence movement as far as slavery and freedom were concerned.

After the Declaration was written and America was preparing to fight for freedom, many African Americans argued that the citizens of America were contradicting themselves, that everything the Declaration proclaimed was a contradiction because many of the people who were fighting for independence from England had slaves. They argued that men who were fighting for freedom, and claiming that they were slaves of Britain and sick of living under tyranny, were treating the slaves they had exactly the same way. The Declaration says that "all men are created equal." Did this only pertain to people of a certain race, wealth, and ethnic background?

This is the question African Americans asked. Many slaves took advantage of this hypocritical and contradictory mentality to advocate what they wanted from the revolutionary process. They wrote petitions to the government in Boston, Massachusetts, and in some other states to argue and advocate their beliefs. Most of their petitions went to Boston because that is where the House of Representatives was and it's where they hoped to be heard. These petitions were sent on numerous occasions (Jan. 6, 1773, April 20, 1773, May 25, 1774, Jan 13, 1777). African Americans pointed out how dangerous and contradictory it was for whites to shout "Liberty or Death" while "enslaving 750,000 human beings." As one petition declared to Boston on April 20, 1773, there are inalienable rights which "as men, we have a natural right to."

There were also some whites questioning the contradiction that was going on, although there were very few. One of these people was Abigail Adams, who told her husband John Adams, a leading American Revolutionary and future American President that, "It always appeared a most iniquitous scheme to me to fight ourselves for what we are daily robbing and plundering from those who have as good a right to freedom as we have."

As the Revolutionary war started to take its course, most white revolutionaries did not want African Americans - free or slave - to bear arms for fear of a black revolt. George Washington at first was against having slaves fight for America. Washington feared that "arming the slaves would lead to conspiracies and insurrections," according to Peter M. and Mort N. Bergman (authors of The Chronological History Of The Negro In America.) This immediately changed once Washington heard of Lord Dunmore's (the governor of Virginia) proclamation on November 7, 1775, which caused much concern among the patriots. The proclamation went as follows, "'I do hereby...declare all indentured servants, Negroes, or others (appertaining to rebels) free, that are able and willing to bear arms, they joining his Majesty's troops, as soon as may be, for the more speedily reducing this Colony to a proper dignity."[1] With the Dunmore proclama-

1 Franklin, John Hope, From Slavery to Freedo

tion the British reminded African Americans that "their masters, though fighting for' Liberty,' still were slave-owners," said Weisberger. Within weeks hundreds of slaves ran away from their masters to fight for the British.

Before Washington resorted to enlisting slaves, many people urged African Americans not to join Dunmore's forces because "British motives were entirely selfish."[2] African Americans were also "promised good treatment if they remained loyal to the Virginia patriots."[3] On December 31, 1775, Washington started to enlist African Americans into his armies because Dunmore's army was increasing and becoming stronger. Like Dunmore, Washington promised freedom to any slaves who would fight for the patriots. Eventually there were African Americans (both free and slaves) fighting for either side. It is said that about 5,000 total African Americans fought for American Liberty. More blacks fought on the British side than the American side, because neither the Congress nor the states were excited to see blacks bear arms. In my opinion, America had no real choice in enlisting Black soldiers. If it had not done so it would have been outnumbered by the British army which was becoming bigger and bigger.

As Washington was enlisting slaves, there were some states such as Virginia who were opposed to allowing their slaves to fight and become free. This started a lot of controversy, yet these states were not left with options. Either Washington would recruit these slaves to fight or many would run away to fight for him so they could get freedom. According to Hope, Jefferson "estimated that in 1778 alone more than thirty thousand Virginia slaves ran away."

During this time many slaves tried to take advantage of the war and the chaos it created to run away completely and become free. Most of them tried to cross the border into Canada, where they could have their freedom

2 Franklin, John Hope, From Slavery to Freedom
3 Franklin, John Hope, From Slavery to Freedom

and be out of reach of the Americans, the British and the war altogether (for the most part). Many slaves started their own settlements in Nova Scotia. Some slaves found refuge among the Indians.

The only reason why African Americans fought in this war was so they could gain liberty for all African Americans. They didn't really care who they fought for or why they were fighting, the only thing that was important was achieving their freedom. As Hope said, "They wanted human freedom as well as political independence." He goes on to say, that a group of African Americans "expressed their astonishment that colonists could seek independence from Britain yet give no consideration to the slaves pleas for freedom." Herbert Aptheker author of <u>Essays in the History of the American Negro</u> says, that slaves had "one set purpose, the achievement of liberty. This was and is the American Negro's guiding star."

There is great irony in the Revolution war. As Lerone Bennett, Jr., author <u>of Before the Mayflower: A History of the Negro in America</u> said, "Consider the background of that great event. A colony with a half-million slaves decides to go to war in support of the theory that all men are created equal and are 'endowed by their Creator with certain unalienable Rights, that among these are Life, Liberty and the pursuit of Happiness.'" Blacks fought for something such as liberty, that was deprived from them for many years. The irony is that "Black men toiled and fought so that white men could be free," says Bennett. As Harriet Beecher Stowe said "It was not for their own land they fought, not even for a land which had adopted them, but for a land which had enslaved them, and whose laws, even in freedom, oftener oppressed than protected. Bravery, under such circumstances, has a peculiar beauty and merit."

Now, the big question is whether or not African Americans got what they wanted. Many believe that African Americans did not reach their destination in receiving freedom. Out of a population of two and a half million people, 500,000 of them were African Americans. Gary B. Nash author of <u>The American People</u> says, "Many of the slaves who fled behind English lines, however, never won their freedom. At the end of the war, as the British prepared to evacuate the port cities, blacks from the surrounding countryside crowded in, begging to be taken away." The slaves were pleading for their liberty but the British were specifically told by the peace treaty to leave quickly without "carrying away any Negroes or other property of the American Inhabitants." When the war had ended, according to Nash, "hundreds of slaves were returned to their American owners. Several thousand others, their value as fieldhands too great to be ignored, were transported to the West Indies and the harsher slavery of the sugar plantations. It was evident that England had not entered the war to abolish slavery." Some of the blacks who fled and found places among the Indians were returned to their masters for money or goods, while others were "held in slavelike conditions by new Indian masters," says Nash. Nash goes on to say, that "Of the blacks who served the Patriot cause many received the freedom they were promised. The patriotism of countless others, however, went unrewarded." The ultimate goal to end slavery had not been accomplished.

Of course there is an opposing side which feels that African Americans did accomplish and gain things from this event. To start, more than 100,000 African American slaves acquired their freedom from this war. According to Aptheker, at least 100,000 slaves ran away. Several thousand left with the British and some slaves found sanctuary in Indian settlements. Even though this might seem very insignificant compared to the population of two and a half million people, it's a beginning. You have to start somewhere. As Hope said, "Negroes made literally scores of such representations and, in so doing, contributed significantly to broadening the ideology of the struggle to include at least some humane freedom as well as political independence." "What the Revolution did was to create space and opportunity for blacks to begin making demands of white society," claims Howard Zinn author of A People's History Of The United States.

I really agree with Zinn, Hope and the many others who feel that the Revolutionary war was a starting point for African American's struggle for equality and sense of freedom. After the war many states started to abolish slavery, most of them were Northern states. By 1810 1/4 of the black population there were still slaves. I agree that these are not the greatest circumstances, but the conditions did improve. Things don't just happen at the snap of a finger, it takes time.

Masters started to free their slaves, like Philip Graham. He freed his slaves in 1778 with the feelings that, "fellow men in bondage and slavery is repugnant to the golden law of God and the unalienable right of mankind as well as to every principal of the late glorious revolution which has taken place in America." Another former master Richard Randolph said, "With regard to the division of the estate, I have only to say that I want not a single Negro for any other purpose than his immediate liberation. I consider every individual thus unshackled as the source of future generations, not to say nations, of freemen; and I shudder when I think that so insignificant an animal as I am is invested with this monstrous, this horrid power."

In the South many slave owners thought slavery was wrong and horrible. In 1782 the Virginia legislature passed a law which allowed slave owners to free their slaves. Within 8 years 10,000 slaves were given their freedom. Pennsylvanians remembering their struggle with England said in their preamble how they wanted to give a proportion of their freedom to others, "who, though of a different color, are the work of the same Almighty hand."

The Revolutionary war changed the mentality of many people when viewing African Americans. Maybe their status wasn't drastically changed, but their participation alone is a big step towards achieving their goals, liberty, equality and justice. I would like to conclude by saying that African Americans did a lot of work for very little, but it was a step towards a whole new revolution. As Hope remarked, "The fact remained, as Edmund Morgan has observed, that to a large degree' Americans bought their independence with slave labor.' It was yet to be seen if human freedom in general was as dear to them as political independence."

Before the American Revolution what we now know as the United States of America consisted of only thirteen out of the present fifty states, and they were called the thirteen colonies. Under the rule of the British, the world's most powerful empire at the time, the thirteen colonies were expected to comply with the laws, rules, and regulations that were set forth by the Parliament in Great Britain. These laws included the Navigation Laws, the Stamp Act, and the Quartering Act.

The Navigation Laws, were solely created in favor of the British, and stated that "No goods or commodities...No sugar, tobacco, cotton, wool, ginger, indigoes, and dyeing wood of the growth, production, or manufacture of any English plantation...shall be shipped anywhere except to another British plantation or to the British Isles." (Excerpts from Navigation Laws, 1660–1696) This broke down the colonies' plantation economies because it hindered them from trade with multiple countries and from making more of a profit off of their products by making them widely accessible.

Navigation Laws were especially appalling to the colonists who were wealthy and wanted to mass-produce their manufactured goods. For example, the Hat Act stated that colonists could not manufacture their own hats. They had to have the cotton shipped to England where it would be manufactured; then the hats would be sold back to the colonies. This act was designed solely to profit England's economy. Both laws also helped the British to profit more off of the colonists' slave labor than the colonists themselves did.

The Stamp Act was a law that stated that anything that had to do with or was made from paper, such as documents, certificates, bills, cards, and newspapers, should have a sales tax placed on them, which made them more expensive to purchase. The colonists had no choice but to still buy and sell these items with the British tax on them because paper goods were a necessity in their business world. This tax hurt everyone besides the slaves. The more transactions that occurred, the more money had to be paid to Parliament.

To help see to it that these laws were carried out, British soldiers were stationed at different places in the thirteen colonies; this was required by the Quartering Act.It seemed as though these British "law enforcers" were causing more problems than they were solving. They were raping colonial women at will, and were constantly getting into confrontations with the people of the land, especially the northern residing colonists. All of these taxes from the British and conflicts with the British soldiers began to mount up until a group of colonists from the city of Boston felt that they could not bear it anymore. What followed were two key breaking points in the relationship between the colonists and the British, which ultimately lead to the American Revolution, the Boston Massacre and the Boston Tea Party.

The Boston Massacre was an event in which an unarmed mob tried to prevent British soldiers from taking their jobs, because "the soldiers began to take the jobs of working people when jobs were scarce." (A People's History of the United States, pg. 66) The mob "began to taunt a British sentry' on duty...in the crowd of soldiers and the mob. Five shots were fired. Five Americans were killed as a result of the gunfire." (How and Why: The American Revolution)

By this time, because of an activist group called the Sons of Liberty, the colonists were so fed up with the British that they did not want any thing to do with them. The Sons of Liberty consisted of middle/upper class workers who made such a big deal out of the massacre that the people living in the colonies that had no problem with England before it now felt that it was now necessary to rebel against the mother country. They released a picture made by Paul Revere depicting a line of British soldiers firing rifles at unarmed colonists. Although the colonists were unarmed, the picture did not show any of their aggression, which historians agree was part of the conflict. More of the people living in the colonies were riled up and were now willing to do anything to break from the bondage of England. The conflict between the Sons of Liberty and the English authorities led some other colonists, who were not yet against British rule, to realize that a bigger fight with England was necessary.

What caused the Boston Tea Party was when England, through the Tea Act, lowered the price of its tea to make it more affordable and to put the colonial tea smugglers that imported their product from the Dutch out of business. Parliament was losing money, but made sacrifices, yet the colonists still fought against it. In the Boston Tea Party the upset colonists, mostly consisting of the Sons of Liberty, raided an English ship that was used to import tea to the colonies and poured 10,000 pounds worth of tea into the Boston harbor. This showed that the Sons of Liberty, who deemed themselves the voice of all the people, felt so strongly against the British that they did not even want to make deals or compromise with them. They had begun to blatantly disobey the laws of Parliament and now were at the point where they hated the British so much that they would revolt against them and declare war if they felt it necessary.

The Tea Act directly hurt the business of the colonial tea smugglers, but not the average colonist. Actually, the Tea Act saved the average colonist money, unlike some of the other Acts. However, the repercussions of the Boston Tea Party was what turned everyone against the British. Since the Tea Party was "the first deliberate, open, violent defiance of British rule" (The American Revolution, pg. 53), Parliament felt the need to punish all the colonists for a select few person's wrongdoings by closing all Boston ports. They introduced the Coercive Acts which not only hindered, but completely stopped oversea and boat trade between Boston and the other colonies or anywhere else. Also "The Royal governor took control over the Massachusetts government and would appoint all officials. Sheriffs would become royal appointees, as would juries. In addition, the British took the right to quarter soldiers anywhere in the colonies" (Coercive Acts Imposed by the British, http://www.multied.com/Revolt/Coercive.html). The soldiers personally affected everyone in the colonies by their presence alone. It was at this point that the Sons of Liberty knew they had the support of the majority of the people in the colonies.

The laws/acts were to be passed to raise more money for England to defend, protect and secure the colonies and its plantations; so they said. Not only did these laws reduce the wealthy colonists' income, they earned the British extra money at the colonists' expense. The British made themselves seem more politically acceptable to the world because they banned slavery in their country, but they were still making money from slavery in America through these taxes. The more money a person made, ideally the more slaves that person would own, which lead to more product produced, and the more taxes they would have to pay. So these laws affected the rich much more than any other class in the colonies and they were the most powerful. Therefore, they felt that they were the ones that would have to lead the other colonists in the revolution against the British.

If the colonists managed to break away from the British successfully the rich would control the land. This was a given, so the country could start off right and not immediately be in financial debt and not have enough money to support all of the people living there. The Boston Massacre and the Boston Tea Party were purposefully provoked by the rich and the Sons of Liberty to get all of the middle class colonists riled up and ready to protest against England in the American Revolution. If the rich had not made the first move I don't think anything would have ever been done about what the Parliament was doing to its colonies. The Coercive Acts were the major breaking point that followed the Tea Party and turned the regular people of the land completely against the British.

The middle class white population could not take as many risks, chances or be as bold in the fight towards freedom as the rich could because they had too much to lose. Most owned farming plantations with few slaves. This was their life and only means of income, yet from it they still only made just enough to support their families. When the Stamp Act, Quartering Act and Navigation Laws were passed, they mildly affected the middle class. They were not large property owners like the rich because they did not own as many slaves, so they didn't have to pay as much in taxes as the rich; but they still had to pay the same percent off of the little product that they were making. The stationed soldiers bothered the middle class because they were strongly influenced by the upper class. Also, the mob that led to the Boston Massacre consisted of mostly middle class individuals who believed, as did the rich, that the British were treating them as slaves. The Boston Tea Party did not bother many in the middle class because for the most part they were not the ones smuggling and trading tea with illegal countries, but the Coercive Act following it "blew their lids" because they too were punished as if they had committed the crime.

The lower classes, which were made up of servants, poor workers and African American slaves and freemen, really did not care about most of the trade laws that were passed. They did not own land or businesses and had very little, if any, money. They were not taxed or economically restricted because they were not selling anything. They were producing but not selling what they produced. If anything, they would be happy that they got to do less work because their masters or employers would not be selling as much as they normally would without laws such as the Stamp or Tea Acts. I assume that the majority of the people in these classes were not fully aware of the details of the taxes or the specifics of the Boston Massacre or the Boston Tea Party. Since many of them could not read (the literacy rate was about 65% of the white men in the cities, according to Pauline Maier) the only way they could know about these events was by word of mouth. If they were slaves, they would likely overhear a master talking about them or hear about them from a slave or servant who traveled or could read.

What would have bothered the slaves about these events was the fact that an African American freeman named Crispus Attucks was one of the men shot and killed during the Boston Massacre. However, many may not have known this because Paul Revere, who illustrated the event in an engraving for the Sons of Liberty, altered the truth to make it seem as though all of the people that were killed were white men. This is clear from a look at that engraving.

The only British laws that had a direct impact on the rest of the lower classes were the Quartering and Coercive Acts. The Quartering Acts hurt the lower classes because the British soldiers who occupied the colonies first of all took jobs away from them. A broadside written in New York in 1770 by Isaac Lamb describes how the people of New York City are falling into poverty and going hungry because some "sell out" businessmen are hiring British soldiers for lower wages. This broadside led to a riot in New York between poor workers and the British soldiers six weeks before the Boston Massacre happened over similar issues.

The Quartering Act also led to the lower classes resenting the soldiers' "police brutality," which happened because it was only natural that armed British soldiers would treat unemployed Americans, who were angry with them for economic reasons, with no respect. This anger at British soldiers had to be widespread because it led to riots in two major cities in a short period of time. When the Coercive Acts increased the power of these soldiers and cut off all Bostonians from trade, the lower class anger there spread to include the entire British government.

Some might argue that the British needed to impose these laws because that is what a government does and needs to do to keep all of its colonies in order. They might also say that British government protected the colonies and allowed a great deal of freedom, including the freedom to protest the British. Finally, they might claim that lots of colonists didn't necessarily support independence. These arguments seem persuasive but they ignore a number of important things. First, those same laws that "needed" to be passed upset upper, middle, and eventually even lower class colonists and made them feel as if they themselves were "slaves of England." The colonists felt as if they were being bound down by an overwhelming number of restrictions called taxes, which caused them to make less money, be less diverse with their sales, and hindered them from mass producing most of their goods. It was not that these colonists were packs of greedy, money-hungry men that constantly rebelled against Parliament. They were just frustrated by what they saw as the inconsiderate and oppressive actions of the British government towards them. They felt as though they were being ruled under a dictatorship by Parliament, which had never imposed direct taxes before the 1760s and which denied them any representatives that could defend their interests and help resolve unfair laws instead of using violence. These issues led to the American Revolution in which the colonists fought the British for independence from 1775 to 1783.

On the whole, I believe that these colonists were right and that the American Revolution improved the lives of the majority of Americans. First of all, the majority of the country was and always has been made up of Caucasian people. At that point in time the upper and middle classes were almost entirely white and I believe that the majority of these two classes united because the middle class felt that the upper class would not do anything to hurt the country and its economy because this would damage everybody. There were about three million people in the thirteen colonies and Caucasians made up almost eighty per cent (Larry Cuban, The Promise of America). Therefore, even if all the enslaved African Americans had joined the British (which they did not - according to Gary Nash, an equal number of African American fought on both sides during the war) the Caucasian majority favored the Revolution, which, by giving that majority the freedom from England they wanted, improved their economic opportunities and therefore their lives.

Second of all, many people in the lower classes did have an interest in the Revolution. Before and during that Revolution, many members of the lower classes participated in the fight against England. They were there at the Golden Hill Riots in New York and at the Boston Massacre. They fought in George Washington's Continental Army. They even demanded in petitions such as the one written by African Americans in Massachusetts in the 1777 and 1778, that the governments that replaced the British during the war give them freedom and education (Herbert Apthekar, editor, <u>Documentary History of the Negro People</u>).

Finally, a country that runs on its own rules and controls its own economy is most of the time much more prosperous. This is because it does not have to deal with direct pressure from another country that promotes different interests through laws and how it believes the country it dominates should be run. Without England's control, the colonists were able to expand America's borders and give land to people who otherwise would have been lower class workers. Without the Navigation Laws, America was able to build industry and become a world power. With a Constitution that gave every citizen equal rights (at least on paper), America created laws that groups who did get great benefits at the time of the Revolution were able to use later on. Today, in comparison to other former British colonies that got their independence much later on (India, the West Indies, and even Canada), America is a much richer, more powerful nation with more economic opportunity.

Some would say that the American Revolution didn't improve the lives of most Americans because it didn't give freedom and power to non-Caucasians and it limited the power of some lower class Caucasians. However, there is a first step for everything and history, especially American history, has shown that nothing happens overnight and that you can't please everyone at the same time. The Revolution laid a foundation of equal rights that most Americans at one point or another have demanded for themselves, even though the government has sometimes denied these rights to many minorities living here. Therefore, I feel that history proves the colonists had valid reasons for wanting to break away from British rule and create their own system, which made the country stronger and improved the lives of most people residing in America in the short and for some the long run.

WAS THE REVOLUTION NECESSARY?
AMERICAN HISTORY
SOCIAL STUDIES PROFICIENCY

A revolution is a big democratic change in a country that deeply affects a country's system of laws and people living in it. In 1776 the Americans had their revolution because they didn't want to be owned by England anymore and follow its rules. They wanted to be their own country and be free from the British law. However there were people who opposed to it, especially some of the rich people because they made money through the English, and the Loyalists who agreed with everything that England was doing to America.

Were the people living in the thirteen colonies right to start a revolution? And was the revolution necessary? This is the question this paper will explore.

I think that the revolutionaries were right and the revolution was the right thing to do at that time because it freed the Americans from Britain. Americans deserved the freedom to trade with other countries. British soldiers had no right taking their jobs and living in their houses. Taxation without representation was unfair. Whatever tax they paid, the Englishman got that money. England lived off everything that the Americans made. British benefited from every law that they made for the thirteen colonies and the Americans suffered for it.

First there was the complete unfair system of taxing. An example of this was "The Stamp Act." It taxed "colonial imports," but that wasn't enough for England. Now they imposed the kind of tax that had long been used in England. Under the Stamp Act British taxed all sorts of things that the colonies used even when they weren't imported. "To show that you paid this tax, you had to buy specially stamped paper. A stamp had to be put on nearly every piece of printed material in daily use: on newspapers, magazines, calendars, receipts etc...If your paper did not have a stamp they would seized you and you would be fined or jailed" (A History of United States by Boorstin and Kelly).

That was so unfair. It wasn't enough that you paid for the newspaper or magazine you had to pay for the stamp too. I can understand the rich doing this, but what about the poor people? The English used money from this tax to payoff its war debt. Why should some other country live off the American taxes? How desperate for money can you be? People started getting angry and "hundreds of merchants in New York City, Philadelphia and Boston agreed not to buy imported goods until the Stamp Act was repealed"(A History of United States by: Boorstin and Kelly). Basically the British could tax or not tax the colonist and the colonist had no say in this. They were right when they stopped buying supplies and started protesting, sometimes violently. Thanks to that the taxes were brought down. However the only way for change to happen was through violence, which was completely unfair.

Second, to enforce the custom and tax laws, the British sent soldiers to the colonies, which abused and harassed the revolutionaries. That was done though the Quartering Act. Americans were supposed to provide food and rooofs over the soldier's heads. They started living in their homes, taking their jobs and on top of that raping their women. " The armies brought a specific terror to American women who were subjected to repeated rapes by British troops stationed in the area"(Women in the Revolution by: Mary Beth Norton).

Britain was a Big Empire and was supposed to protect the colonies from their enemies not hurt them. At the same time in NYC the British wanted to destroy the Liberty Poles that the colonists were putting up. The Poles were put up as symbols at resistance to the British oppression. They didn't really succeed the first couple of times. They destroyed an inn known to serve anti- British New Yorker's. The soldiers "Smashed eighty-four of the inn's windowpanes, plus lamps and bowls" (Battle of Golden Hill by: Richard Ketcham) and when the people heard about it. They got angry at both the British and the people who employed soldiers to work for them instead of hiring the needy poor. New Yorkers paid taxes to support them and that was how they showed how grateful they were.

The colonists got really angry and decided to finally do something about it. They agreed on "condemning the soldiers and the Quartering Act"(Battle of Golden Hill). The big fight took place on the Golden Hill where many soldiers were killed and badly bruised. After everything went back to place they called it" The Battle of the Revolution"(<u>Divided Loyalties</u> by: Richard Ketcham).

Those were the beginnings of disagreements between the British soldiers and colonists, when American people started realizing that they were "free born Englishmen" but not Americans. They had the right to fight for their freedom and their property. They gave the troops everything but since they didn't appreciate that they had to show them that they had no right destroying the American property. Perhaps some innocent people died but it was worth it. They got their point across. But again, the only way to win was through violence, which was not how anyone else would not want to live.

Third, England "started meddling inside the colonies,"(<u>A History of United States</u> by: Boorstin and Kelly) trying to take control of everything, especially things colonists made money from. When the British banned the colonies from importing tea and made them buy the British tea the Americans really got angry. The Americans didn't want to drink the English tea for two reasons: " it cost more than the smuggled Dutch tea, and it's price included the only part of the Townshend taxes that had not been repealed"(<u>American Revolution,</u> Robert Sobel), but it also gave more power to the British. " The colonists also objected that the government was shrewdly trying to gain implicit acceptance of Parliament's taxing power by offering tea at a reduced price. They knew that if they would drink that they would also be swallowing the English right to impose taxes again. (<u>The American People</u> by: Howard Zinn).

But they weren't so naive and started opposing everything that England had to offer. When the ships from London came to deliver the tea the colonists would either send them back or dump the tea in to the water as they did in The Boston Tea Party. "When the Americans were asked to pay for the tea that they dumped and refused the government was forced to close the port. ("The Colonizing People" in <u>The American People</u> by Gary Nash). But still the people didn't want to pay anything because it was unfair; they didn't want that tea there in the first place they started protesting. When the Americans didn't buy their tea, the economy in Britain was in trouble. The Englishmen started losing money, which was so important to them.

It was the right thing to do; they wanted their freedom and had to get it somehow. If violence was the key they did the right thing in using it. It leads to a revolution but for a good cause. They were free from British taxes and British laws.

Charles Inglis was one of the loyalists who presented strong arguments about not having a war with Britain. First he said in a document called "The True Interest of America Impartially Stated." "By a connection with Great Britain, our trade would still have the protection of the greatest naval power in the world. Past experience shows that Britain is able to defend our commerce and our coasts; and we have no reason to doubt of her being able to do so in the future." All he is saying is that since Britain had this great power and the largest navy, America can have its' protection. But he is also implying that America will suffer without England to protect it. However, if America is ready to fight for independence, it is certainly ready to protect itself from enemies. In addition if most of America's taxes went to the English and America was under Britain's laws, the English had to protect them. They were living off the colonies.

Secondly he says "Whilst connected with Great Britain, we have a bounty on almost every article of exportation; and we may be better supplied with goods by her, than we could elsewhere". This is not necessary a true statement. England was taxing them for those goods and the people paid much more money than I think was necessary.

The tea that England sent them they didn't want to buy. They smuggled cheaper Dutch tea and other products that they thought were better from what the English had to offer. England also didn't allow the colonies to manufacture many products. If the colonists could manufacture their own products maybe they wouldn't have to rely on England for "better products".

Thirdly Charles Inglis says that if Americans fight "Devastation and ruin must mark the progress of their war along the sea coast of America. Ruthless war, with all its aggravated horrors will ravage our once happy land our seacoasts and ports will be ruined, and our ships taken. Torrents of blood will be split, and thousands reduced to beggary and wretchedness." He makes a good argument here, but as I said at the beginning violence always was the answer to the colonists' problem. Violence was a necessity to get rid of The Stamp Act, The Quartering Act and many other laws. Even then, the British would not cooperate. War at that time was the right thing to do. Yes, people had to die but thanks to that, America became independent and was able to establish laws and taxes that did suit them and were best for them.

Finally Inglis said, "The Declaration of Independence on the part of America, would preclude treaty entirely; and could answer no good purpose. We actually had already have every advantage of Independence, we should instantly lose assistance from our friends in England." How can he say that the colonies already had their freedom? If they did they wouldn't be complaining in the first place. The colonists were not satisfied with the decisions and laws that Britain put upon them. That's why they wanted the war. Otherwise the British were not listening and didn't really care what the American people wanted. They were making money and paying their debts. What else could they want?

The people living in the colonies were right to start a revolution. They finally became free from England and were able be in charge of their own country.

CHAPTER NOTES FOR TEACHERS

Inquiry teaching assumes the teacher is always on the lookout for new materials that engage students in historical research and present new perspectives on historical issues. For that reason, any list of resources is subject to change, including the list below. But I hope my suggestions will help you get started on your own inquiry.

These sources are listed by chapter heading; some are annotated with references to specific documents discussed in the text.

Introduction
Loewen, James, *Lies My Teacher Told Me*, Touchstone Press, 1995

Chapter 4 The Missing Slavery Clause
Nash, Gary, *Race and Revolution*, Madison House, 1990
For the "Seneca Falls Sentiments": Foner, Philip, *We the Other People, Alternative Declarations of Independence*, University of Illinois, l976
For Frederick Douglas's analysis of July 4th: Mullane, Deirere (ed.), *Crossing the Danger Water*, First Anchor, 1993

Chapter 7 The People
Boorstin , Daniel, et al., *A History of the United States,* Ginn and Co. 1983
Gilje Paul, *The Road to Mobocracy,* University of North Carolina Press, 1987
Zinn, Howard, *A People's History of the United States*, Harper, 1980
For Declaration of the Stamp Act Congress: *Proceedings of the Congress of NY*, Annapolis, 1766

Chapter 8 The Boston Massacre

Hakim, Joy, *From Colonies to Country,* Oxford Press, 1993

For the British high school textbook: Holley, Erica, *How and Why: The American Revolution,* Trafalgar Square, 1986

For the pamphlet by 3 Bostonians sympathetic to American cause, excerpts from letters by British commander, and John Adams's court summation: *The American Revolution: Opposing Viewpoints,* Greenhaven Press

For Paul Revere's engravings: New York Historical Society archives

Chapter 9 The Golden Hill Riots

Burrows, Edwin and Wallace, Mike, *Gotham: A History of New York City to 1898,* Oxford Univ. Press, 2000

Ketchum, Ralph, *Divided Loyalties: How the American Revolution Came to New York,* Henry Holt & Company, 2002

For the broadsides by the Sons of Liberty and British soldiers: New York Historical Society archives

For Boyer Lee R., "Lobster Backs, Liberty Boys, and Laborers in the Streets: New York's Golden Hill and Nassau Streets Riots": *New York Historical Society Quarterly,* 57 (1973)

Chapter 10 The Boston Tea Party

Morgan, Edmund, *The Birth of the Republic: 1783-1789,* University of Chicago Press, 1986

Nash, Gary, *The American People: Creating a Nation and a Society,* 1986

Sobel, Robert, *The American Revolution,* Ardmore Press, 1967

Zinn, Howard, *A People's History of the United States,* Harper 1980

For "Resolutions of the New York Sons of Liberty" see www.patriotresource.com

Chapter 11 George Washington

Brookhiser, Richard, *Rediscovering George Washington, Foundation Father,* Free Press, 1996

Ginsberg, Eli and Eichner, Alfred, *The Troublesome Presence: Democracy and Black Americans,* Transaction Publishers, 1993

Quarles, Benjamin, *The Negro in the Making of America* (3rd ed.), Touchstone Press, 1996

Raphael, Ray, *A People's History of the American Revolution*, Perennial, 2002

Wiencek, Henry, *An Imperfect God: George Washington, His Slaves, and the Creation of America*, Farrar, Straus & Giroux, 2003

Zinn, Howard, *A People's History of the United States,* Harper, 1980

For an Englishman's view of Washington: Pious, Richard, *Young Oxford Companion to the Presidency of the United States*, Oxford University Press, 1995

For the collection of Washington's documents published by the National Center for History in the Schools: Nash, Gary (ed.), *The Great Experiment, George Washington and the American Republic,* 1999

For Phyllis Wheatley's poem and letter and for Washington's reply to Wheatley see *The Black Presence in the Era of the American Revolution* by Sidney and Emma Kaplan, University of Mass. Press, 1989

Chapter 12 Thomas Jefferson

Bowers, Claude, *The Heritage of Jefferson,* Workers Schools, 1943

Hakim, Joy, *A History of US*, Oxford University Press, 2002

Hemmings, Madison *Thomas Jefferson and Sally Hemmings: An American Controversy,* University of Virginia Press, 1997

Jefferson, Thomas, *On Democracy,* ed. by Saul K. Padover, Penguin 1946

Jefferson, Thomas, *Notes on the State of Virginia,* Library of America, 1984

Maier, Pauline, *American Scripture: Making the Declaration of Independence,* Alfred Knopf, Vintage, 1998

Nash, Gary, *The American People,* Harper Collins, 1990

Schlesinger, Arthur, Jr., *Thomas Jefferson, The American Presidents Series,* Henry Holt, 2003

Wilkins, Roger, *Jefferson's Pillow: The Founding Fathers and the Dilemma of Black Patriotism,* Beacon, 2001

Wills, Gary, *The Negro President: Jefferson and the Slave Power,* Houghton Mifflin, 2003

For *Founding Slaveowners,* see *Emerge Magazine,* George Murray 1992

For *Washington Post* article on conference on Jeffersonian Legacies: "Thomas Jefferson, Tarnished Icon?" *Washington Post,* Oct. 17, '92

For *The New York Times* article by Orlando Patterson, "Jefferson the Contradiction":
The New York Times, Nov. 10, '98

For Jefferson's correspondence with Benjamin Banneker and Jefferson's letter about
Banneker: see *The Black Presence in the Era of The American Revolution,* Sidney and
Emma Kaplan, U of Mass Press, 1989

Chapter 13 African Americans and the American Revolution

Apthekar, Herbert, *A Documentary History of the Negro in the United States,* Citadel
Press, 1963 (for documents written by African Americans in Massachusetts)

Apthekar, Herbert, *The Negro in the American Revolution,* International Publishers,
1964

Franklin, John Hope, *From Slavery to Freedom,* Alfred Knopf, 1967

Nash, Gary, *Race and Revolution,* Madison House, 1990

Chapter 14 Native Americans and the Revolution

Nash, Gary, *The American People,* Harper & Collins, 1990

Chapter 15 Women's Role in the American Revolution

Lerner, Gerda, *The Woman in American History,* Addison-Wesley Publishing Co., 1971

Norton, Mary Beth, *Liberty's Daughters,* Little Brown & Co., 1980

For profile of Abigail Adams, John Adams's reply to Abigail Adams and her complaint to Mercy Warren: see Hymowitz, Carole and Weiss, Michaele, *A History
of Women in America,* 1978

Chapter 16 The Working Class and the Revolution

Apthekar, Herbert, *The American Revolution,* International, 1960

Lemisch, Jesse, *The American Revolution Seen From the Bottom Up,* 1967

Linebaugh, Peter, and Rediker, Marcus, *The Many-Headed Hydra,* Beacon 2000

Zinn, Howard, *A People's History of the United States,* Harper, 1980